the **COOKBOOK** *for teens*

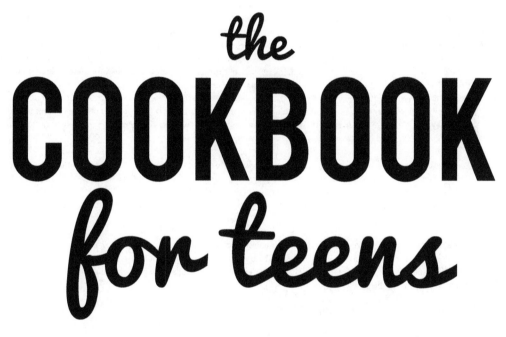

the
COOKBOOK
for teens

The Easy Teen Cookbook with
74 Fun & Delicious Recipes to Try

MENDOCINO
PRESS

Contents

Introduction

You're getting older—a definite perk that means more opportunities, but also more responsibility. You're learning new skills as you make more mistakes. (It's impossible to do one without the other.) One of these days in the not-so-distant future, you will be living on your own (and, in doing so, will gain a much deeper appreciation of everything your parents ever did for you). Along with learning how to choose the right water temperature for the washing machine when doing your laundry (hot wash? cold rinse?), and replacing the toilet paper when it runs out, you will also be largely responsible for cooking and keeping yourself fed. Waiting until you're on your own and it's midnight and your stomach is rumbling isn't the best time to open a cookbook for the first time. Necessity may be the mother of invention, but it can also create some burned—and terrible tasting—food. Not to mention an even louder and emptier stomach.

While you're still living at home, where your family will forgive you if you mess up a recipe and will make sure you don't starve, why not learn the basics of cooking? In case you haven't already guessed, that's what this book is for. It has been written to help you learn what you need to fend off hunger, and even impress your family and friends in the process.

In these chapters, you will learn how to read a recipe. You'll find out about basic cooking techniques, how to plan a meal from the first course through the last, what to keep in your kitchen cupboards and refrigerator, and how to turn a recipe into a shopping list. You'll even discover how to navigate the grocery store, shop for bargains, and know when to say yes—or no—to buying organic. You will learn that a pastry brush is not for painting portraits of chefs, and that there's a difference between "1 cup nuts, chopped" and "1 cup chopped nuts."

Best of all, you will realize that cooking, for the most part, is simpler than you thought, and certainly way more fun. Want a bonus? How about a little peace of mind? With the lessons you find in this book, you will not only be able to defeat your own hunger—before and after school, on the way out the door to work, in the middle of an all-night study session, or while relaxing on weekends—but you'll also be able to impress a girlfriend/boyfriend, "bribe" your parents, or please your friends. No more showing up at parties without something to contribute. No more scrambling for something other than a sealed jar of olives when unexpected company stops by. No more opening the refrigerator door ten times in a row just to close it again because you couldn't find anything good to eat.

You've got it covered—you know how to cook!

PART ONE

Cooking Basics

CHAPTER ONE

You're the Chef

So many types of food—yet so little time! If you're going to take charge in the kitchen, don't be surprised if you feel exhilarated, enthusiastic, *powerful*—and completely intimidated. Where to start? What to make first? How to choose?

All of those questions are normal, and there is no single correct answer. What you decide to make first depends on your personal preferences. Are you more interested in cooking or baking? What kinds of foods do you like to eat? What are some of your family's favorite dishes? All of these questions need to be taken into consideration when choosing what to make.

One piece of advice is true throughout, however: *Start simple.* If you wanted to race bicycles professionally one day, you wouldn't start out by trying out for the Tour de France, one of the hardest bike races in the world. You would start by riding in your neighborhood, learning new skills and tricks where it's safe to practice, and if you messed up, a video of it wouldn't end up online in a matter of minutes. The same is true with cooking. Start simple, and then build your skills as you get more familiar with measuring, mixing, and preparing.

As you delve into the world of cooking, you will first need to learn how to read a recipe. While it can seem like they are written in some kind of foreign language, recipes actually are pretty easy to understand once you learn the basics.

Let's look at some of the terms that might be confusing. Some of them refer to cooking methods, while others are general terms typically used in many recipe directions. Look through this list. The terms in bold are ones that will be explained in further detail within the chapters.

TERM	DEFINITION
Braise	To cook food slowly in a small amount of liquid in a tightly covered pan on the stove
Boil	To heat a liquid to the point when large bubbles rise to the surface of the liquid and make quite a bit of noise
Broil	To cook food at very high temperatures below direct, dry heat. The top oven rack is usually placed in the highest position to be close to the broiler (although some ovens are equipped with drawer-type broilers beneath the oven itself).
Brown	To cook meat until brown—no longer pink or red—on the outside
Chop	To cut foods with a knife into smaller pieces
Fold	To gently combine a lighter mixture into a heavier one so they are properly mixed
Fry	To cook food in hot cooking oil or other melted fat, usually until browned and crisp
Grate	To rub food (hard cheeses, vegetables, etc.) against a grating surface to make fine, small pieces
Grease	To coat a surface or pan with a thin layer of oil, butter, or other fat, typically before baking
Grill	To cook food by placing it on a grill rack directly over a heat source; often done outside with charcoal
Knead	To press and work dough with the heels of your hands
Low/medium/ high heat	The level of heat over which a food is cooked, whether a gas flame or a heating element
Mince	To chop food into very fine pieces
Preheat	To turn on the oven to a specified temperature before you start making the recipe. The oven needs a few minutes to heat up to the proper temperature before you put the food in.
Roast	To cook meat uncovered in an oven using a dry-heat cooking method

Sauté	To cook food in a small amount of fat or water over fairly high heat in an open, shallow pan
Season with/ to taste	Most recipes use the term "to taste" when including spices in the ingredients list, or use "season with" in the directions. Basically it means to add however much you personally like! Some people like lots of salt and pepper; others not so much. Not sure how much you want to use? Taste the spice lightly on your finger and see how much you like it. Start light—you can always add more when you make the recipe again.
Serves __ / Makes __	This states how much food a recipe will yield. "Serves" indicates how many people the recipe will serve as an appetizer, entrée, dessert, or side. "Makes" indicates the total amount of finished food the recipes will yield (such as for a sauce or dip). If you're cooking for more or fewer people than indicated by the recipe's yield, you will need to multiply or divide the ingredients to adjust to your needs. Or just make extra for leftovers or to share with friends.
Simmer	To heat a liquid to the point when small bubbles rise to the surface of the liquid fairly rapidly but don't make much sound
Steam	To cook food in the hot water vapor given off by boiling water
Stir continuously	Stir without pausing for as long as indicated in the recipe
Stir frequently	Stir fairly often for as long as indicated in the recipe, but not to the point that you're stirring without stopping
Tender	For vegetables, this is when you can poke them with a fork and the tines slide easily into the flesh. For pasta, tender is when you bite into it and it's easy to chew, but firm (not mushy), and has no taste of flour.
Translucent	The color of the food (usually onions) as it changes from solid to transparent during cooking
Zest	The colored outer portion of citrus fruit peels (lemon, lime, oranges, etc.). Removed with a grater, the zest is full of oils and flavor, and can be used as seasoning. The white pith, which lies beneath the thin layer of zest, is very bitter and should not be used for cooking or seasoning.

Once you've chosen what to make, and you know how to read and speak "Recipe," sit down and read through the ingredients and directions from beginning to end. Are you confused by anything in the recipe? If so, stop and figure out the problem long before you have a pot bubbling on the stove or the oven preheating.

Here are some additional tips that can make recipes easier to understand:

1. Ingredients are listed in the order they will be used as you make the recipe.
2. The order of the words in an ingredients list provides clues as to what to do. If the list says, "1 cup chopped nuts," that means you chop nuts until you have a full cup of them. If the recipe says, "1 cup nuts, chopped," that means you first measure 1 cup of nuts and *then* chop them up.
3. Once you've made a dish a few times, the measurements for certain things, like seasoning, can be adjusted, but the first few times you make a recipe, follow the listed measurements exactly.
4. Don't grab a regular drinking cup or soup spoon for measuring ingredients. These won't give you accurate measurements. Use measuring cups and spoons calibrated specifically for cooking so you know you're using the right amounts.

Planning Ahead

By this point in your life you've certainly learned that planning ahead is a smart thing to do in general! You study and do your homework in preparation to perform well on tests. You practice your sprints, eat healthy food, and get plenty of rest before a track-and-field competition. You go over the packing list before heading out to hiking camp (realizing you forgot something while high up on a butte, six miles from your campsite—not fun).

The same rule applies to cooking. By reading through the recipe and making sure you understand it, you've taken the first steps. Take a few more by checking that you have the cooking tools and ingredients you need to prepare the dish.

What if there is a special occasion coming up and you want to do something a little fancier than fixing yourself a quick lunch or making a simple casserole for the family? Can you plan out an entire meal with several courses, from start to finish, and then cook and serve it? Of course you can—as long as you remember to plan ahead.

Planning for a Three-Course Meal

Yeah, cooking three courses does sound a little overwhelming—but not if you break them down into their separate components. Usually, a three-course meal is divided up into an appetizer (usually a soup or salad), a main course (or "entrée"), and a dessert. See? It already sounds easier, right?

To make sure your meal is impressive rather than embarrassing, here are a few tips to keep in mind:

- Select your recipes ahead of time, and be sure they are ones you've made before and feel comfortable making. In this book, the suggested menu combination is:

Course 1
Soup: Call-It-Flower Soup (p. 61)
OR
Salad: Bacon Drizzle Salad (p. 58)

Course 2
Main Course: Simple Shepherd's Pie (p. 91)

Course 3
Dessert: Luscious Lemon Bars (p. 115)

- Do your grocery shopping at least one day before you are going to cook. That way if you forgot something, or didn't get enough of it, you still have time to run out and get it.
- Check to make sure that none of the people you are cooking for have food allergies, sensitivities, or preferences you should know about. If your meal is centered around a meat dish, for example, and you discover at the last minute that one of your guests is a vegetarian, it could be awkward. The same is true if you prepare something guests really don't like or that could cause a harmful physical reaction!

As you look through the recipes in this book, and in other resources, don't reject one just because it has an ingredient in it you don't like. Most of the time, you can get around that ingredient by either leaving it out entirely or replacing it with something you prefer. For example, if a recipe calls for walnuts and you hate them—but you love pistachios— then use pistachios instead of walnuts. If the recipe uses grape juice and you really prefer cherry, go ahead and swap them. Not an olive fan? Use something else or leave the olives out. Many of the recipes you will find here offer a number of options, so you can choose which ones you like (or rule out which ones you don't like).

Now, get into that kitchen. It's time to learn a new skill—and luckily, there are no tests or grades involved!

CHAPTER TWO

Making the Kitchen Yours

You've planned out the meal—it sounds absolutely delicious.

You've read the recipes—they sound pretty simple.

It must be time to start cooking, right?

Well—no, not quite. You've learned a lot, but you still have to take a few very important steps.

Even the best recipe coupled with the best techniques won't work if you don't have the necessary tools and ingredients waiting for you in the kitchen. It isn't much fun to be halfway through a recipe only to find you're missing a key ingredient (just imagine pizza without any cheese!) or that your little sister used the measuring spoons to feed her fish and now they're sitting at the bottom of the aquarium.

Let's first take a look in your kitchen's drawers and cupboards and find the equipment you need to have ready and waiting. Then, we'll go over the supplies you'll want to have stashed away in the pantry and in the refrigerator before you put on your apron (although you don't have to wear one if you don't want to). We'll also talk for a moment about cooking safely. You wouldn't want to ruin all of your fun and hard work by either preparing a meal that ends up making you sick or by using tools that send you to the emergency room for stitches.

Just the Basics

You may not own a mandoline slicer, pastry brush, garlic grater, or empanada press—but you don't have to. Many people get along just fine without these tools, and unless you're planning to become a professional chef, you aren't likely to need them, either. Instead, here's a list of what you will most likely need in the kitchen:

- Can opener
- Bottle opener
- Grater
- Mesh sieve (a metal strainer with many small holes)
- Colander (a bowl-shaped strainer with small holes for washing and draining foods)
- Wooden spoon
- Slotted spoon (a spoon with a few holes or slits in it)
- Measuring spoons
- Measuring cups
- Mixing bowls (glass, ceramic, or stainless steel)
- Sharp chef's knife (a 6- to 10-inch knife used for a variety of cutting tasks, such as chopping and mincing)

- Sharp serrated knife (a knife with a sawtooth edge, good for cutting things like bread and tomatoes)
- Whisk
- Tongs
- Spatula
- Pie pan
- Baking sheet (also called a cookie sheet, baking tray, or sheet pan)
- Large nonstick skillet with lid
- Small nonstick skillet with lid
- Large saucepan with lid
- Small saucepan with lid
- Ovenproof casserole dishes with lids
- Timer
- Meat thermometer
- Cutting board
- Dish towels
- Oven mitts/pot holders

What? Your small nonstick skillet doesn't have a lid? Your dad's set of tongs broke last week? The dish towels are all in the laundry? No need to panic. This is the *ideal* list—if you're missing something, chances are you'll still be able to make every dish in this cookbook. If not, no worries—you'll just do a little improvising.

Time to Shop!

Recipe? Check.
Equipment? Check.

Now it's time to make sure you have the ingredients you'll need to start cooking. What you'll want to buy will depend on what you're planning to make and what kind of food you like—and don't like. If you're a vegetarian, for example, skip past the recipes with meat. If you like to bake, pay closer attention to those recipes.

First, see what ingredients your chosen recipe requires. Next, check to see what you already have in the kitchen—not just in the refrigerator and freezer, but in the cabinets, too. Whatever you need, but don't already have, goes on your shopping list.

As you write your list, organize the foods in groups of similar items. Put all of the produce items together, as well as the meat, dairy products, and grains. It will make shopping much faster, and you will spend less time backtracking from one section of the store to the other. Then list each group in the order you will encounter them, if possible. For example, if the produce section is right inside the front door, put those items on the top of the list. It may take you a few more minutes to do this when writing the list, but you will more than make up for it when you are going up and down the aisles of the grocery store in a flash.

As you walk into the store, have your list in hand (no point in making it and then leaving it on the kitchen table!). Never do your shopping when you're feeling hungry—you will buy more, and often on impulse—you don't *need* those Froot Loops! Stick to your list. You can save money at the grocery store by buying in bulk, seeking out sale items, and using newspaper and online coupons.

If you're doing a general shopping trip so that you have the ingredients for making multiple recipes, what should you buy? Here is a general list of items to have on hand.

Vegetables and Fruits

If the fruit or vegetable you're looking for is not in season, and either isn't in the store or is incredibly high-priced, consider buying it frozen. It's often just as healthy—and flavorful. Just make sure that whichever frozen fruit you buy doesn't contain added sugar and that your frozen vegetables are free of extra "sauces," sodium, or other flavorings or additives. Canned fruit and vegetables can also be good choices. Just check the ingredients list and try to select brands that are low in sodium (salt) and sugar.

- Apples
- Avocados
- Bananas
- Beans (canned kidney, black, lima, and garbanzo beans can easily go into a number of dishes)
- Berries
- Broccoli
- Carrots
- Cauliflower

- Corn
- Garlic
- Grapes
- Lemons
- Mushrooms
- Onions
- Oranges
- Potatoes (white and sweet)
- Tomatoes

When Is It Ripe?

Do you ever have trouble trying to figure out if a piece of fruit is ripe? You're not alone. For some fruit, the key is the color. For example, you can look at a banana skin and if it's green—not ripe! Yellow? Ripe. Yellow with brown spots? At the peak of ripeness. For other fruit, such as cantaloupe, ripeness can be determined by smell. Press on the stem end, and if you can smell cantaloupe, it's ripe! For some other fruits, ripeness means degree of firmness. A pineapple should be firm, but not hard as a rock. (It's fruit, not a weapon!) The same is true for avocados. Peaches are ripe when they yield ever so slightly when you press them (but don't squeeze too hard, or you'll bruise the fruit).

Pantry Items

Here are some of the basic ingredients you'll need to make everything from brownies to pancakes:

- Baking powder
- Baking soda
- Bread
- Chocolate chips
- Cocoa powder
- Flour (white and whole wheat)
- Honey
- Nuts (almonds, walnuts, pecans)
- Pasta
- Rice (white or brown)
- Rolled oats
- Sugar (white granulated, brown, and confectioners')
- Vanilla extract
- Yeast

Dairy Products

- Butter
- Cheese
- Eggs
- Milk
- Yogurt

Meat and Poultry

- Bacon
- Chicken breasts and/or thighs
- Ground beef
- Pork chops
- Sausage links
- Turkey breast cutlets

Going Organic

Are organic fruits and vegetables worth the extra cost? It depends. If you're concerned about the final cost at checkout, then stick with what's on sale. If you're worried about chemicals or know you're sensitive to them, then organic might be a better choice.

Condiments, Sauces, Oils, and Vinegars

- Barbecue sauce
- Chicken stock or broth (a great base for many recipes)
- Ketchup
- Mayonnaise
- Mustard
- Olive oil
- Salsa
- Spaghetti sauce
- Vegetable oil
- Vinegars (apple cider, rice, balsamic)

Herbs and Spices

Be sure to have a wide variety of herbs and spices on hand, as they provide the key flavor to a number of dishes. Always have the following on hand:

- Black pepper
- Chili powder
- Cumin
- Garlic powder
- Ground cinnamon
- Rosemary
- Salt
- Thyme

After shopping with these lists, you will have a very complete and well-stocked kitchen. The time to start cooking is incredibly close, but don't jump into the recipe just yet. Instead, do your homework on how to have fun in the kitchen *and* stay safe at the same time.

Safety First!

The kitchen is the place where you can create amazing masterpieces, delicious dishes, and rockin' recipes. Unfortunately, it's also a place where you can get hurt. Cooking and baking involve the oven and stove top—which means open flames, hot burners, or a hot oven. Protect yourself from potential burns by following just a dozen simple rules.

Always...

1. Use a dry pot holder or oven mitt when working with hot pots or pans.
2. Keep your face and arms back from hot pans to avoid the chance of a steam burn.
3. Turn your face away when opening a hot oven.
4. Keep your hair tied back, if your hair is long.
5. Make sure pot handles are turned in toward the stove so they can't be hit or get caught on clothing.
6. Stir slowly and carefully when working with hot food.
7. Make sure appliances like blenders and food processors are unplugged before you add ingredients. Once the ingredients are in, plug in the appliance and turn it on. Turn it off and unplug it again before removing the food.
8. Wipe up spills as soon as they occur.
9. Take spoons and other utensils out of hot pans.
10. Make sure no water comes near hot oil when frying food.
11. Keep motorized appliances (blenders, food processors, etc.) away from water.
12. Stay focused on what you are doing—cooking is not the place for distractions.

Potential danger in the kitchen is also found in the multiple sharp blades you'll be handling. It might be the blades at the bottom of a blender or the serrated knife you use to slice bread. It could be the vegetable peeler with which you're skinning potatoes or the grater you need to use for shredding cheese. Each one of these tools can slice skin just as quickly as it does food, so it's *essential to be extra careful* when using them. Unless you're cooking for vampires, no recipe is enhanced by blood, and it's hard to concentrate on measuring and stirring if you're busy searching for bandages and antibiotic cream.

A sharp knife is safer than a dull one. It will cut faster and easier, and you will be less likely to push hard and slip. If you have a knife sharpener, use it carefully (or have an adult help you) to ensure your blade is as sharp as possible. When using a knife of any kind, keep the sharp edge pointing down toward the food. Hold the handle (never, ever the blade) with four fingers, while using the other hand to anchor the food you're cutting so it doesn't slide, slip, or roll off of the cutting board.

How you hold the knife is only one part of keeping safe when using it, however. If you need to walk across the room with it, make sure the blade is pointed toward the floor. Even after you have put a knife down, a blade can be dangerous. Never put it near the edge of the counter where it might easily be knocked off. If it does start to fall, don't even think about trying to catch it. Let it go, but get your toes out of the way. Don't put a dish towel or oven mitt on top of a knife, either—it's too easy to reach for the towel and catch the blade as well. Do not put a dirty knife into a sink of soapy water. It would be far too easy to reach in and accidentally cut yourself.

Graters and vegetable peelers also carry a risk since they have sharp edges. When using a grater, stop when the food you are grating is getting too small to safely hold. Otherwise, you could end up getting some skinned knuckle in your recipe. When using a peeler, hold it firmly and always push it away from you. As with knives, don't place these sharp tools in a sink full of soapy water or dishes, where they can hide and end up hurting you.

An Invisible Danger

One of the biggest dangers in the kitchen is one you can't even see: bacteria. It can creep in when the juices of raw meat encounter other ingredients, subsequently contaminating your food. It can occur when cold food gets too warm, warm food gets too cold, or a combination thereof. Bacteria is also a threat when food is not cooked to the appropriate temperature. In any of these cases, your dish can result in people getting sick instead of thanking you for a tasty treat.

How can you make sure this invisible threat doesn't show up as an unwanted guest in your kitchen? Here are the basic common-sense rules to follow:

1. *Always* wash your hands in hot, soapy water before you start to cook.
2. Make sure the kitchen is clean before you begin. Wipe off countertops and be sure your cutting boards are clean.
3. Wash your hands after handling any type of raw meat.
4. Do not use the same knife and cutting board for raw meat that you use to prepare other ingredients. Knives and cutting boards must be very thoroughly washed after touching raw meat.
5. If you need to thaw meat for a dish, do so overnight in the refrigerator, not on the countertop at room temperature.
6. If food is perishable, do not allow it to be at room temperature for more than two hours. During hot weather, it should not be out for more than one hour.
7. Learn how to cook meat to the appropriate and safe temperature (see the following chart). To be sure it is cooked, insert a meat thermometer into it and check that it has reached the right temperature. Ground meat, poultry, chicken, and turkey should not have any pink color, and juices should run clear when you cut into the meat.

MEAT COOKING CHART

Meat	Temperature
Beef, pork, veal, lamb (ground)	160°F
Turkey, chicken (ground)	165°F
Beef, veal, lamb (steaks and chops)	145°F
Poultry	165°F
Pork and ham	160°F
Fish	145°F

After figuring out what tools you need, what ingredients are required, and how to stay safe in the kitchen, you're definitely ready to start. You have made the kitchen yours, and now it's time to put it all to use and create culinary masterpieces—or at least have some fun!

PART TWO

Recipes

CHAPTER THREE

Breakfast

Some people think of breakfast as a luxury to be saved for lazy weekend mornings, but many health experts believe it's the most important meal of the entire day. Before heading out for a busy day of school, work, sports—or even just some fun with your friends or family—eat a good breakfast full of vitamins, minerals, and protein. It will help give you the energy to power right through the day!

19

German Fruit Bowl

SERVES 3 TO 4

This big German pancake makes the perfect bowl for your favorite type of fruit. To ensure this dish turns out correctly, pay extra attention to keeping the oven and the pan at the right temperature before adding the batter.

Be sure to use an *ovenproof* skillet here so you don't ruin your pan or the oven. Most stainless-steel, anodized-aluminum, and cast-iron skillets are safe for the oven. Any pan with a wooden or plastic handle, or coated with a nonstick coating (such as Teflon), is *not* ovenproof.

1 TABLESPOON UNSALTED BUTTER

4 EGGS

1 CUP WHOLE MILK

½ TEASPOON VANILLA EXTRACT

1 CUP ALL-PURPOSE FLOUR

¼ TEASPOON SALT

MAPLE SYRUP, FRESH FRUIT, APPLESAUCE, OR OTHER TOPPING, FOR SERVING

1. Preheat the oven to 450°F.

2. Place the butter in an ovenproof skillet and put it in the oven while you make the batter.

3. Crack the eggs into a large bowl. Using a whisk, whip the eggs until they are frothy. Next, add the milk and vanilla and whisk well. Add the flour and salt and stir until smooth.

4. Once the oven has preheated, use a pot holder to remove the skillet and set it on the stove top. Pour the batter into the hot skillet and place it back in the oven. Bake until the pancake is puffy and golden brown at the edges, about 15 minutes.

5. Remove the skillet from the oven (don't forget that pot holder!) and let the pancake cool for 1 minute. It will deflate like a balloon! Finally, add your favorite topping, such as maple syrup, fresh fruit, or applesauce, and then slice the pancake into wedges and serve.

Tropical Morning Milkshake

SERVES 1 TO 2

This drink is quick and easy to make, and it's full of minerals, including calcium and potassium. It tastes just like a milkshake, but without tons of sugar and calories.

1 BANANA, PEELED

1 CUP UNSWEETENED VANILLA ALMOND MILK

1 CUP UNSWEETENED COCONUT WATER

¼ CUP PINEAPPLE JUICE

¼ TEASPOON GROUND CINNAMON

½ TEASPOON VANILLA EXTRACT

HANDFUL OF ICE

Place all the ingredients in a blender. (Remember to keep it unplugged until the lid is on and you're ready to hit the button.) Blend on high for 30 seconds. Turn off—and unplug—the blender, and then pour your milkshake into a glass (or two) and enjoy!

Breakfast

Good-for-You Muffins

MAKES 12 MUFFINS

Muffins have a pretty bad reputation these days, but they can be made into a healthy option for the morning. Check these out.

BUTTER, FOR THE PAN

3 EGGS

⅓ CUP SUGAR

½ CUP VEGETABLE OIL

1 CUP GRATED APPLES

1 CUP GRATED CARROTS

1 CUP WHOLE-WHEAT FLOUR

1 CUP ALL-PURPOSE FLOUR

1 TABLESPOON BAKING POWDER

¼ TEASPOON SALT

½ TEASPOON GROUND CINNAMON

½ TEASPOON GROUND ALLSPICE

1.   Preheat the oven to 375°F. Butter a 12-cup muffin pan or use paper liners.

2.   In a large bowl, combine the eggs, sugar, and oil and stir until smooth. Stir in the apples and carrots.

3.   Into another large bowl, sift together both flours using a sieve or sifter. Add the baking powder, salt, cinnamon, and allspice. Add the wet ingredients to the bowl with the dry ingredients, a little at a time, and stir until well combined.

4.   Spoon the batter into the prepared muffin pan. Bake for 25 minutes or until golden brown. Serve with butter or your favorite jam.

Seedy Parfait

SERVES 3 TO 4

Packed with protein, this power breakfast makes boxed cereals look like cardboard and fluff. When this homemade granola is added to yogurt, a delicious parfait is the result.

3 CUPS ROLLED OATS

⅓ CUP UNPROCESSED, COARSE BRAN

⅓ CUP SESAME SEEDS

⅓ CUP RAW HULLED SUNFLOWER SEEDS (SEE NOTE)

½ CUP HONEY OR MAPLE SYRUP

1 CUP COARSELY CHOPPED PECANS OR WALNUTS

¼ TEASPOON GROUND ALLSPICE

¼ TEASPOON GROUND CINNAMON

2 CUPS MIXED RAISINS, DRIED CRANBERRIES, AND CHOPPED PITTED DATES

½ CUP TOASTED WHEAT GERM

3 CUPS YOGURT OF YOUR CHOICE

1.   Preheat the oven to 350°F.

2.   In a large bowl, combine the oats, bran, sesame seeds, and sunflower seeds. Spread the oat mixture evenly on a baking sheet and bake for 15 minutes, until golden brown. Leave the oven on.

3.   In the bowl you used for the oat mixture, combine the honey, nuts, and spices. Stir in the hot oat mixture until well coated.

4.   Return the mixture to the baking sheet, spreading it out into an even layer. Bake the granola, stirring every few minutes, until it is brown all over, about 10 minutes. Pay close attention while it cooks—it burns easily!

5.   In a large bowl, toss the granola with the dried fruit mixture and the wheat germ and set aside to cool.

continued ▶

6. Place a spoonful or two of yogurt in a parfait glass. Spoon some of the granola on top. Alternate layers of yogurt and granola until you get to the top of the glass. Repeat the process in two or three more glasses, or save the leftovers in an airtight container to make more parfaits another day.

Note: "Hulled" means the sunflower seeds have been removed from their shells.

Mini Muffin Pizza

SERVES 1

Who doesn't love pizza? You can make it for breakfast, and it can be both healthy and delicious.

1 WHOLE-WHEAT ENGLISH MUFFIN, SPLIT IN HALF
1 SMALL TOMATO, DICED
1 TEASPOON OLIVE OIL
1 SLICE CANADIAN BACON, DICED
¼ CUP SHREDDED MOZZARELLA CHEESE
A FEW FRESH BASIL LEAVES, CHOPPED

1. Preheat the oven to 400°F.

2. Cover a baking sheet with aluminum foil. Place the muffin halves cut-side up on the sheet. Top both halves with diced tomatoes and drizzle the olive oil on top. Add the Canadian bacon pieces and sprinkle the cheese on top.

3. Bake the pizzas for 10 to 12 minutes, until the cheese has melted and is starting to brown. Finally, carefully remove the pizzas from the oven, sprinkle the basil on top, and enjoy!

Breakfast

Buenos Días Burrito

SERVES 1

Add a little taste of Mexico to your morning with this simple and fast treat.

½ TEASPOON BUTTER OR OIL

2 EGGS

1 TORTILLA (WHITE OR WHOLE-WHEAT)

¼ CUP SHREDDED CHEDDAR OR MONTEREY JACK CHEESE

¼ CUP DRAINED AND RINSED CANNED BLACK BEANS

¼ CUP FRESH SALSA

½ AVOCADO, SLICED

½ CUP SOUR CREAM

⅛ TEASPOON GROUND CUMIN

1.   In a skillet, melt the butter over medium heat. Crack the eggs into a bowl and beat them together with a whisk. Pour the eggs into the skillet. Using a wooden spoon or spatula, stir the eggs around the pan to scramble them (1 to 1½ minutes should be about perfect). Remove the pan from the heat and set aside.

2.   Set the tortilla on a plate and put the hot eggs in a line down the middle of the tortilla. Sprinkle on the cheese and black beans, and then add the salsa and avocado slices. Top with sour cream. Sprinkle with the cumin. Roll up the tortilla, folding in one end so all of the tasty ingredients don't fall out. Time to eat! *Buenos días!*

Sweet Sunrise Scones

SERVES 3 TO 4

Did you think scones were too fancy to make at home? Think again! With this accessible recipe, you can bring a teatime elegance to your mornings.

BUTTER OR OIL, FOR THE PAN

¼ TEASPOON GROUND CINNAMON

½ TEASPOON SUGAR

1½ CUPS WHOLE-WHEAT FLOUR, PLUS MORE FOR DUSTING

½ CUP CORNMEAL

1½ TEASPOONS BAKING POWDER

1½ TEASPOONS BAKING SODA

¼ TEASPOON SALT

½ CUP CHOPPED PECANS OR WALNUTS

½ CUP RAISINS

⅓ CUP MAPLE SYRUP

¾ CUP PUMPKIN PURÉE (SEE NOTE)

1 EGG, LIGHTLY BEATEN

¼ TEASPOON VANILLA EXTRACT

¼ CUP ORANGE JUICE

1.   Preheat the oven to 400°F. Butter or oil a baking sheet. In a small bowl, combine the cinnamon and sugar; set aside.

2.   In a large bowl, mix together the flour, cornmeal, baking powder, baking soda, salt, pecans, and raisins.

3.   In a separate large bowl, combine the maple syrup, pumpkin, egg, and vanilla and stir well.

4.   Add the wet mixture to the bowl with the dry mixture and stir until they form a firm dough.

continued ▶

5. Sprinkle some flour on a flat surface. Take half of the dough out of the bowl and knead it about five times. Roll the dough into a ball. Using the palm of your hand, flatten the dough into a 1-inch-thick disk. Cut the disc into 8 equal-size triangles—these are your scones. Repeat with the remaining dough—you will have 16 scones total.

6. Place the scones a few inches apart on the prepared baking sheet. Using a pastry brush, brush each piece of dough with orange juice. Finally, sprinkle the cinnamon-sugar mixture evenly over the scones.

7. Bake for 8 to 10 minutes. To make sure they are done, stick a toothpick in the middle of one of the scones. If it comes out clean (meaning, there are no crumbs or other bits stuck to the toothpick), the scones are ready.

Note: Be sure to use canned pure pumpkin, not pumpkin pie mix, which has spices and sometimes other flavorings added.

How to Knead

What does it mean to knead the dough? Although each cook may describe the process a little differently, here are the basic steps:

1. On a lightly floured work surface, form the dough into a ball and press down on it to flatten it. Push it away from you, using the heels of your hands.

2. Fold the dough back onto itself, turn it 90 degrees (this is called a "quarter turn"), and repeat. Keep doing this for the time specified by the recipe, usually between 5 and 20 minutes.

3. If the dough is too sticky, add a little flour to your work surface and put a thin coating of vegetable oil on your hands.

4. The dough is properly kneaded when it feels smooth and springs back when you press your fingertip into it.

High-Rise Hero

SERVES 1

Who said sandwiches are only for lunch? Why not build a breakfast sandwich? You can add whatever you want to it, which is why the ingredients list has so many choices!

½ TEASPOON BUTTER

1 EGG

1 SLICE SWISS, AMERICAN, CHEDDAR, MOZZARELLA, OR MONTEREY JACK CHEESE

1 ENGLISH MUFFIN, HAMBURGER BUN, BAGEL, OR CRUSTY ROLL

AVOCADO SLICES, TOMATO SLICES, LETTUCE, MAYONNAISE, MUSTARD,
    FOR TOPPING

1 OR 2 SLICES DELI HAM, TURKEY, BEEF, SALAMI, OR CHICKEN

1.   In a skillet, melt the butter over medium heat.

2.   Crack the egg into the skillet and fry for 2 to 3 minutes, flipping the egg halfway through cooking so the yolk breaks and the egg is evenly cooked.

3.   Place your chosen slice of cheese on top of the egg for just long enough to slightly melt the cheese; then slide the egg and cheese onto the bread.

4.   Add the rest of your toppings, and then sink your teeth into your own personal high-rise hero.

Breakfast

Going Coconuts

SERVES 2 TO 3

Coconut products, including coconut water, juice, and milk, are becoming extremely popular—and for understandable reasons. They are packed with potassium and magnesium and have a light, sweet taste. Here is a great way to add coconut to your morning meal.

This dish is easy to change—if you hate apples, but love grapes, go ahead and use grapes. Make it your own! If you like soupier, creamier fruit salad, you can add more coconut milk. If you like it drier, use less.

1 APPLE, CORED AND CHOPPED

1 BANANA, SLICED

1 ORANGE, PEELED AND SECTIONED

⅓ PINEAPPLE, PEELED, CORED, AND CHOPPED

½ CUP NUTS (SUCH AS ALMONDS, WALNUTS, PECANS, OR HAZELNUTS)

½ CUP COCONUT MILK, OR AS NEEDED

In a large bowl, combine the apple, banana, orange, and pineapple. Add the nuts and coconut milk and stir.

Deep-Dish French Toast

SERVES 2 TO 3

This is a very rich breakfast, so don't plan to make it often. However, when you do, enjoy every second of it. Since this dish must sit in the refrigerator overnight, plan to start the night before. You will be glad the next morning that you did.

2 TABLESPOONS PLUS 1 TEASPOON BUTTER

⅔ CUP PACKED DARK BROWN SUGAR (SEE NOTE)

2 TABLESPOONS HONEY

1½ CUPS MILK

1 TEASPOON VANILLA EXTRACT

¼ TEASPOON SALT

1 TEASPOON ORANGE FLAVORING (SEE NOTE)

GRATED ZEST OF ½ ORANGE

3 EGGS

6 THICK SLICES BREAD

6 TABLESPOONS FROZEN WHIPPED TOPPING (SUCH AS COOL WHIP), THAWED

2 TABLESPOONS FINELY CHOPPED PECANS

6 ORANGE SLICES

Breakfast

1.   Grease the bottom of a 13-by-9-inch baking dish with 1 teaspoon of the butter.

2.   In a small saucepan, combine the remaining 2 tablespoons butter, the brown sugar, and the honey. Cook over medium heat, stirring continuously so the mixture doesn't burn, until it is bubbling and the sugar has dissolved, about 5 minutes.

3.   Carefully pour the mixture into the prepared baking dish, spreading it evenly, and then set it aside to cool.

4.   In a large bowl, combine the milk, vanilla, salt, orange flavoring, orange zest, and eggs. Stir together with a whisk.

5.   Dip one slice of bread in the milk mixture and lay it in the baking dish on top of the cooled butter-sugar mixture. Repeat this process with the remaining bread. Pour any leftover milk mixture on top of the slices. Cover the dish and refrigerate overnight.

continued ▶

Deep-Dish French Toast *continued*

6.   In the morning, preheat the oven to 350°F. Uncover the baking dish and slide it into the oven. Bake for 30 minutes or until the bread is lightly browned. Remove the French toast from the oven and top each slice with some of the whipped topping and pecans, along with a slice of orange.

Note: Brown sugar is usually "packed" into the measuring cup to remove air pockets from the sugar. Since it is slightly damper than regular white granulated sugar, it doesn't settle into the measuring cup quite as nicely. Look in the extracts and spices aisle of the supermarket for orange flavoring.

Sweet Potato–Pecan Pancakes

SERVES 2 TO 3

This recipe combines three tasty foods—pecans, sweet potatoes, and pancakes—into one unique dish. You will need some already cooked sweet potatoes for this, so consider having some sweet potatoes the night before with your dinner, and make a couple of extra ones.

1¼ CUPS ALL-PURPOSE FLOUR

¼ CUP PECANS, CHOPPED

3 TABLESPOONS YELLOW CORNMEAL

2 TABLESPOONS BAKING POWDER

½ TEASPOON SALT

½ TEASPOON GROUND CINNAMON

1 CUP MILK

1 CUP MASHED BAKED SWEET POTATO

3 TABLESPOONS BROWN SUGAR

1 TABLESPOON VEGETABLE OIL

½ TEASPOON VANILLA EXTRACT

2 EGG YOLKS

2 EGG WHITES, LIGHTLY BEATEN

1 TEASPOON BUTTER OR OIL

MAPLE SYRUP, FOR SERVING

Breakfast

1. In a large bowl, combine the flour, pecans, cornmeal, baking powder, salt, and cinnamon, and stir with a whisk.

2. In a separate large bowl, combine the milk, sweet potato, sugar, oil, vanilla, and egg yolks, stirring until smooth.

3. Add the wet mixture to the bowl with the dry mixture and stir until well combined.

continued ▶

Sweet Potato–Pecan Pancakes *continued*

4.   In a third bowl, using a hand mixer, or in the bowl of a stand mixer fitted with the whisk attachment, beat the egg whites on high until soft peaks form. Then slowly fold the egg whites into the batter. Let the batter stand for 10 minutes.

5.   In a large skillet, melt the butter over medium heat. Spoon about one-quarter of the batter per pancake onto the pan. Cook for 2 minutes, until the edges look cooked and bubbles appear on the surface of the pancake. Carefully flip the pancake with a spatula and cook for 2 minutes more. Serve with maple syrup.

Separating Eggs

While most recipes tend to call for whole eggs, you may find that some recipes, like the Potato-Pecan Pancakes, require you to separate the yolk and the white of the egg. How do you do it without getting egg all over your hands, the countertop, and the floor? There are at least a dozen methods people use, but here is the most common:

1. Have two small bowls ready.

2. Break the egg as close to the middle as possible.

3. Hold one half of the shell in each hand, broken-side up, so the eggshell halves are like little bowls. One half should have the egg (or most of it!), and the other should be empty.

4. Holding the halves over one of the small bowls, slowly pour the yolk back and forth from one half to the other, letting the white slide into the bowl below. Be very careful not to break the egg yolk on the edge of one of the eggshells.

5. Repeat the process 3 or 4 times until only the yolk remains in one of the eggshell halves and as much of the white as possible is in the small bowl below. Put the yolk in the empty bowl.

Breakfast

CHAPTER FOUR

Snacks

Uh-oh. It's happening again. That empty feeling. That familiar rumble and growl.

Yes, it's the remarkable time of day known as . . . the Snack Attack! The symptoms often strike right around the time you get out of school and walk through the front door of your house. Thoughts of school, homework, friends, and chores all fade as you think about your increasingly demanding stomach. Lunch was eons ago, and dinner is just floating out there, unseen, in the coming evening hours.

This condition also sneaks up on you on weekends . . . right around midnight. You're almost ready for bed, but wait! Suddenly, food sounds perfect. Cue the rumble and growl!

What can you do to make sure you survive these ruthless Snack Attacks? Your best defense is to get creative in the kitchen.

Most snacks tend to fall into one of two categories: sweet or salty (although the two can be combined to make something delicious!). This chapter contains recipes for some of each, designed to combat even the most powerful attacks.

Vegetable Brownies

Two words you almost never see together are vegetables *and* brownies, *but this recipe manages to combine them. Plus, the brownies are tasty and nutritious. Seriously!*

OIL OR BUTTER, FOR THE PAN

¼ CUP COCOA POWDER

1 CUP WHOLE-WHEAT FLOUR

½ TEASPOON BAKING SODA

¼ TEASPOON BAKING POWDER

⅛ TEASPOON SALT

½ CUP SUGAR

¼ CUP UNSWEETENED APPLESAUCE

¼ CUP VANILLA YOGURT

1 CUP GRATED ZUCCHINI

1 EGG, LIGHTLY BEATEN

½ CUP PECANS, CHOPPED

1. Preheat the oven to 350°F. Butter an 8-inch-square glass baking dish.

2. In a medium bowl, mix the cocoa powder, flour, baking soda, baking powder, and salt. In a larger bowl, mix the sugar, applesauce, yogurt, zucchini, and egg.

3. Next, pour the dry mixture into the wet mixture, and stir until well combined. Stir in the pecans.

4. Pour the batter into the prepared baking dish. Bake for 20 to 25 minutes, or until a toothpick inserted into the brownies comes out clean. Let the brownies sit in the baking dish for a few minutes to cool; then cut them into 16 squares and serve.

Folding Ingredients

Folding is a technique that allows you to blend one mixture into another without losing the air bubbles in the lighter mixture, like fluffy beaten egg whites. It's best to use a metal spoon or rubber spatula to fold ingredients together. Always add the delicate, lighter mixture to the heavier one—not the other way around. Use the spoon/spatula in a cutting motion, cutting through the center of the two mixtures and bringing the heavier one to the surface. Turn the bowl as you do so, rather than stirring. Continue to do this until the mixtures are combined to the point indicated by the recipe, such as "until no white streaks remain" or "until completely combined."

Ice Pop Paradise

YIELD VARIES BASED ON SIZE OF MOLDS

The Popsicles you get at the store often have more sugar and artificial flavorings and color-ings than any other ingredient. You can make your own at home with fruit juice and fruit, which costs less and tastes better. Here is just one possibility.

1½ CUPS SEEDLESS WHITE OR RED GRAPES, HALVED
3 CUPS WHITE OR PURPLE GRAPE JUICE
1½ CUPS CRANBERRY JUICE
CRAFT STICKS (AVAILABLE AT CRAFT STORES)

1. Drop 4 to 6 grape halves into each ice pop mold.

2. Combine the grape juice and cranberry juice in a pitcher; then pour the mixture into the molds almost to the top.

3. Insert a stick into each mold and place the molds in the freezer. Freeze for at least 6 hours, until solid. Before eating, pull out the molds and let them stand at room tem-perature for a few minutes so the ice pops will be easy to remove from the molds.

Humble Hummus

MAKES 1 CUP

Okay, admittedly, hummus looks pretty boring, but try not to judge before tasting it. Hummus is one of the most popular snacks around the world, and now you can make your own and see why so many people like it. This recipe is tasty, but basic, so feel free to sparkle it up by adding extras like roasted garlic, sliced olives, minced sun-dried tomatoes, toasted pine nuts, black pepper, crumbled cheese, or sliced scallions.

ONE 16-OUNCE CAN CHICKPEAS, DRAINED AND RINSED

2 TABLESPOONS OLIVE OIL

2 TABLESPOONS PLAIN YOGURT

1 TABLESPOON LEMON JUICE

½ TEASPOON GROUND CUMIN

½ TEASPOON SALT

¼ TEASPOON GARLIC POWDER (SEE NOTE)

PITA POCKETS AND/OR CHIPS, FOR SERVING (OPTIONAL)

CUCUMBER, CARROT, AND CELERY STICKS, FOR SERVING (OPTIONAL)

1.   In a food processor, combine the chickpeas, oil, yogurt, lemon juice, cumin, salt, and garlic powder and process until very well blended.

2.   Transfer the hummus to a serving bowl or platter and spread it on pita bread or chips, or use it as a dip for the chips or veggie sticks.

Note: At the supermarket or when you're hunting around in the spice cabinet, be sure you're grabbing garlic *powder*, not garlic *salt*. Garlic powder is ground dehydrated garlic, while garlic salt is salt with a little garlic powder added for flavor. Using the wrong one will definitely put an unwelcome salty spin on your hummus!

Wrap It Up!

SERVES 2

Tortillas can make fast, delicious snacks out of whatever you might have in the kitchen. Try them with peanut butter and jelly, with cheese and apple slices—or in this recipe.

2 WHOLE-WHEAT TORTILLAS
4 TABLESPOONS CREAM CHEESE
4 SLICES DELI HAM (OR YOUR FAVORITE DELI MEAT)
1 SMALL RED BELL PEPPER, SEEDED AND CUT INTO THIN STRIPS
5 GREEN OLIVES, CUT INTO THIRDS

1.   Place one of the tortillas on a large plate. Spread 2 tablespoons of the cream cheese over the tortilla, leaving a 1-inch border around the edges. Place 2 slices of ham on the tortilla, and then add half of the pepper strips and half of the olives. Roll up the tortilla and repeat with the other tortilla.

2.   Cut each rolled tortilla into four pieces and serve.

42

Sweet Potato Surprise

SERVES 4

You already know that potatoes make tasty French fries. Believe it or not, so do sweet potatoes, and they have slightly fewer calories, too.

4 SWEET POTATOES
½ TEASPOON GROUND CINNAMON
2 TABLESPOONS VEGETABLE OIL
½ CUP SOUR CREAM, FOR DIPPING

1. Preheat the oven to 450°F.

2. Wash the sweet potatoes and pat them dry. Halve each sweet potato lengthwise, and then cut each half into three long pieces. Place all the pieces in a large bowl and sprinkle with the cinnamon and the oil. Stir until they are evenly coated.

3. Place the sweet potato fries in a single layer on a baking sheet and bake for 15 minutes. Take the pan out and flip the fries over. Bake for 15 minutes more. Check the fries—if they are done, a fork should slide easily into them. If they are not quite done, continue baking for 3 to 4 minutes and then check them again. Remove the baking sheet from the oven and let the fries cool slightly. When they are cool enough to handle, serve them with the sour cream for dipping.

Snacks

Popcorn Perfection

SERVES 1 TO 2

Popcorn has a bad reputation—but that's largely because of the heaps of butter and salt many people add to it. Can you have your popcorn and be healthy, too? Of course! Just try this instead. If you like your snack sweeter or more filling, you can replace the spices with nuts, dried fruit, or chocolate chips.

1 BAG PLAIN MICROWAVE POPCORN

¼ CUP GRATED PARMESAN CHEESE

¼ TEASPOON GARLIC POWDER

¼ TEASPOON CAJUN SEASONING OR CAYENNE PEPPER

¼ TEASPOON SALT

¼ TEASPOON GROUND BLACK PEPPER

Pop your bag of microwave popcorn as usual, and then add all of the seasonings (if you don't want to dirty a bowl, you don't even need to take the popcorn out of the bag!). Shake the bag to coat the popcorn in the seasonings, and snack away.

Sweet and Salty Nuts

MAKES 2 CUPS

If you can't decide which you like better—sweet? salty?—how about putting them together and ending the debate? This fast, protein-packed snack can help give you the stamina for an afternoon of homework or a late night up with friends.

1 TABLESPOON BUTTER

2 CUPS SALTED NUTS (A MIX OF YOUR FAVORITES, SUCH AS PEANUTS, CASHEWS, PECANS, WALNUTS, ALMONDS, OR PISTACHIOS)

1 TABLESPOON LIME JUICE

2 TEASPOONS SUGAR

½ TEASPOON SALT

1 TEASPOON CHILI POWDER

1. Preheat the oven to 300°F.

2. In a medium skillet, melt the butter slowly over low heat. Alternatively, microwave the butter in a medium bowl for 30 to 60 seconds to melt it.

3. Next, add the nuts and lime juice to the melted butter. Stir until the nuts are completely coated. Spread the nuts into a single layer on a baking sheet and bake for 35 minutes, until toasted. Stir the nuts a few times while they bake.

4. Remove from the oven, and while the nuts are still warm, sprinkle them with the sugar, salt, and chili powder. Stir well.

Bagel Bakes

SERVES 1

This recipe adapts to your preferences. Feel like you need a sweet treat? Make the first version. Rather have a savory snack? Try the second.

Cin-fully Sweet Bagel Bakes

¼ TEASPOON GROUND CINNAMON
½ TEASPOON SUGAR
1 TABLESPOON BUTTER
1 CINNAMON-RAISIN BAGEL

1. Preheat the oven to 325°F. In a small bowl, combine the cinnamon and sugar. Set aside.

2. In a small skillet, melt the butter slowly over low heat. Alternatively, microwave the butter in a small bowl for 30 to 60 seconds to melt it.

3. Very carefully slice the bagel horizontally into four thin, round pieces. Using a pastry brush, coat the tops of the slices with the melted butter. Sprinkle the bagel slices with the cinnamon-sugar. Place the bagel slices on a baking sheet and bake for 10 minutes.

4. Remove the baking sheet from the oven, flip the bagel slices, and repeat the coating process on the other side. Bake for 10 minutes more and serve. Crunchy sweetness!

Savory Bagel Bakes

3 TABLESPOONS BUTTER
2 CLOVES GARLIC, FINELY CHOPPED
1 PLAIN OR GARLIC BAGEL
1 TEASPOON GRATED PARMESAN CHEESE

1. Preheat the oven to 325°F.

2. In a small skillet, heat the butter with the garlic over medium heat, just until the butter is melted and the garlic is fragrant. Remove the pan from the heat.

3. Very carefully slice the bagel horizontally into four thin, round pieces. Using a pastry brush, coat the tops of the slices with the garlic-butter mixture. Place the bagel slices on a baking sheet and bake for 10 minutes.

4. Remove the baking sheet from the oven, flip the bagel slices, and repeat the coating process on the other side, adding a sprinkle of the cheese to each one. Bake for 10 minutes more and serve. Savory goodness!

47

Snacks

Slammin' Apple Sammies

SERVES 1 TO 2

With plenty of protein and a touch of sweetness, this snack takes care of almost every possible craving!

1 APPLE, CORED AND CUT CROSSWISE INTO 4 ROUND SLICES
2 TABLESPOONS ALMOND BUTTER OR PEANUT BUTTER
½ TEASPOON GROUND CINNAMON
2 TABLESPOONS MINI CHOCOLATE CHIPS

Spread one apple slice with 1 tablespoon of the almond butter. Sprinkle ¼ teaspoon of the cinnamon and 1 tablespoon of the chocolate chips on top. Place another apple slice on top. Repeat with the remaining apple slices, almond butter, cinnamon, and chocolate chips.

Emergency Snacks

What if you can't wait? What if your stomach demands IMMEDIATE filling? In that case, here are some great snacks to have on hand or put together in minutes:

FROZEN GRAPES

PEANUT BUTTER AND CINNAMON ON APPLE WEDGES

NUTS, RAISINS, AND SEEDS MIXED TOGETHER

CELERY STICKS, CARROT STICKS, AND CUCUMBER SLICES
    WITH RANCH DRESSING FOR DIPPING

HARD-BOILED EGGS, SLICED IN HALF AND TOPPED WITH MAYONNAISE,
    HOT SAUCE, OR MUSTARD

CHAPTER FIVE

Salads and Soups

This chapter looks at two of the most basic types of food: salads, which often require far more time for chopping and cutting than actual cooking, and soups, which typically require just the opposite—more cooking time than preparation. Of all the recipes in this book, these are the ones with the most flexibility with ingredients. You don't like one of the toppings? Replace it. You prefer more or less dressing? Adjust it! These dishes are also flexible because you can make them for a side dish, a light lunch, or just a snack. Eat them whenever they appeal the most.

Before you start looking through the salad recipes, remember that there is a *huge* variety of greens out there. So why not give any of the following a try? You can combine them to get slightly different flavors. You should also know that the darker the color of the leaf, the more nutrients it usually has.

Types of greens:

- Arugula
- Cabbage (green or purple)
- Chard
- Dandelion greens
- Escarole
- Kale
- Lettuce (iceberg, romaine, red or green leaf)
- Radicchio
- Spring mix
- Watercress

Also remember that salads come in many different forms, some of which don't have any greens in them at all, such as fruit salads and pasta salads. Check them out, too!

Sweet Berry Salad

SERVES 1 TO 2

Adding fruit to a salad often makes it more appealing—and tastier. You can use any variety of fruit, depending on what's in season and what you like best. This salad uses strawberries, but you can use blueberries, blackberries, raspberries, apples, or whatever you prefer. Feel free to choose the type of nuts and cheese you like best as well. A vinaigrette or poppyseed dressing often works best with this type of salad.

1 CUP GREENS OF CHOICE
½ CUP STRAWBERRIES
⅓ CUP WALNUTS, CHOPPED
⅓ CUP FETA CHEESE, SHREDDED
2 TO 3 TABLESPOONS SALAD DRESSING OF YOUR CHOICE

Rinse the greens and tear them into bite-size pieces. Place them in a large salad bowl. Cut the strawberries into small pieces and add them to the bowl with the greens. Add the walnuts and sprinkle on the cheese. Top with your favorite dressing.

52

Presto! It's Pesto

SERVES 2 TO 3

This filling salad uses pasta to provide its bulk. It tastes fancy, but is simple to make.

3 CUPS UNCOOKED PENNE PASTA

1½ CUPS CHERRY TOMATOES, HALVED

ONE 15-OUNCE CAN WHOLE BLACK OLIVES, RINSED AND DRAINED

¼ CUP PREPARED PESTO (SEE BELOW)

2 TABLESPOONS MAYONNAISE

1 CLOVE GARLIC, MINCED

SALT AND GROUND BLACK PEPPER

FRESH BASIL LEAVES, FOR GARNISH

1. Fill a large pot with water and bring it to a boil. Add the pasta and cook for 12 minutes. Drain and rinse with cold water.

2. In a large bowl, combine the cooked pasta, tomatoes, and olives and toss to combine.

3. In a medium bowl, combine the pesto, mayonnaise, and garlic and stir thoroughly. Pour the pesto mixture over the pasta mixture. Season with salt and pepper, garnish with basil leaves, and serve. (If you're not serving the salad right away, cover the bowl and stick it in the refrigerator to chill.)

Pesto

MAKES ABOUT ⅔ CUP

Want to make your own pesto? Here's how.

¼ CUP ALMONDS

3 CLOVES GARLIC

1½ CUPS FRESH BASIL LEAVES

½ CUP OLIVE OIL

PINCH OF NUTMEG

SALT AND GROUND BLACK PEPPER

continued ▶

Pesto *continued*

1. Preheat the oven to 450°F.

2. Place the almonds on a baking sheet and toast them in the oven for 10 minutes.

3. Transfer the toasted almonds to a food processor or heavy-duty blender and add the garlic, basil, oil, nutmeg, salt, and pepper. Plug in the food processor and process the ingredients into a thick paste. Turn off and unplug the food processor; then carefully scoop out the pesto into a container.

Cuke Connection

SERVES 2 TO 3

This is an example of a very simple salad that has no greens, but is still full of fiber and nutrition.

1 TO 2 CUCUMBERS, PEELED AND HALVED LENGTHWISE
½ RED BELL PEPPER, SEEDED AND CHOPPED
3 TABLESPOONS RICE VINEGAR
1 TABLESPOON VEGETABLE OIL
2 TABLESPOONS SUGAR

1.   Scoop the seeds out of the cucumbers and discard them. Cut the cucumbers crosswise into thin slices and put them in a bowl. Add the bell pepper.

2.   In a small bowl, whisk together the vinegar, oil, and sugar.

3.   Pour the dressing over the vegetables and stir until coated. Cover and chill for 1 hour before serving.

Patriotic Potato Salad

SERVES 6 TO 8

Did you know that potatoes come in different colors? You can be patriotic by making this salad, which uses white- and red-skinned potatoes, plus delicious—and popular—purple potatoes. This salad takes extra time and work, but it will be a definite hit.

1 TEASPOON SALT, PLUS MORE AS NEEDED

½ CUP BROWN SUGAR

1 TEASPOON GROUND CUMIN

GROUND BLACK PEPPER

1 TO 2 VIDALIA ONIONS, THINLY SLICED

1 BONELESS, SKINLESS CHICKEN BREAST, HALVED

½ CUP OLIVE OIL

6 TO 8 RED, WHITE, AND PURPLE POTATOES

1 CUP HEAVY CREAM

1 TEASPOON ONION POWDER

1 CUP WHITE CORN (FRESH OR FROZEN AND THAWED)

¼ CUP CHOPPED FRESH CILANTRO, FOR GARNISH

1.   Preheat the oven to 350°F.

2.   In a small bowl, combine the salt, sugar, and ½ teaspoon of the cumin. Season with pepper to taste. Spread the onion slices in a layer on a baking sheet. Sprinkle them with half of the sugar mixture.

3.   Put the chicken breast halves on top of the onions. Coat both sides with the olive oil, and then sprinkle with the remaining sugar mixture. Bake for 30 to 40 minutes. Allow to cool, then dice the chicken.

4.   Quarter the potatoes and place them in a large pot. Add enough cool water to cover the potatoes by about 1 inch. Bring the water to a boil and cook the potatoes until they can be easily pierced with a fork. Drain and set aside to cool. When cool enough to handle, cut them into bite-size pieces.

5.   In a large bowl, stir together the heavy cream, remaining ½ teaspoon cumin, and the onion powder. Season with salt and pepper. Add the chicken, potatoes, and corn, and stir until coated. Garnish with the cilantro and serve.

Salad in a Glass

SERVES 8

This wonderful salad is tasty—and compact. It has a lot of ingredients, but hang in there. It's worth the time and effort.

1⅓ CUPS UNCOOKED WHITE OR BROWN RICE

¼ CUP OLIVE OIL

¼ CUP LIME JUICE

1 TEASPOON GROUND CUMIN

1 TEASPOON HONEY

1 CLOVE GARLIC, CRUSHED

¼ TEASPOON SALT

¼ TEASPOON GROUND BLACK PEPPER

1 RED BELL PEPPER, SEEDED AND DICED

1 RIPE AVOCADO, PITTED, PEELED, AND CUBED

ONE 14-OUNCE CAN BLACK BEANS, DRAINED AND RINSED

1 MANGO, PEELED AND CUBED

1½ CUPS CORN KERNELS (FRESH OR FROZEN AND THAWED)

1½ CUPS DICED TOMATOES

½ SCALLION, CHOPPED

1½ CUPS GRATED CHEDDAR CHEESE

¼ CUP CHOPPED FRESH CILANTRO

1.   Cook the rice according to the package directions. (Cooking times and water quantities tend to differ slightly between brands, so follow the bag or box.)

2.   Spread the cooked rice on a baking sheet to cool, fluffing it with a fork.

3.   In a jar with a lid, combine the oil, lime juice, cumin, honey, garlic, salt, and black pepper. Seal the jar and shake until the dressing is well mixed.

4.   Layer the rice, bell pepper, avocado, beans, mango, corn, tomatoes, scallion, cheese, and cilantro evenly into eight parfait glasses. Drizzle with the dressing.

Bacon Drizzle Salad

SERVES 2 TO 4

Spinach and bacon salad is a classic in the world of salads. Dress it up a little and make it taste gourmet with this recipe.

½ CUP HALVED PECANS
6 SLICES UNCOOKED BACON, CUT INTO 1-INCH PIECES
1 RED ONION, THINLY SLICED
4 TOMATOES, THINLY SLICED
⅓ CUP WHITE WINE VINEGAR
1 TABLESPOON SUGAR
1½ POUNDS SPINACH LEAVES
SALT AND GROUND BLACK PEPPER

1. Preheat the oven to 350°F.

2. Spread the pecans out on a baking sheet and toast in the oven for 10 to 15 minutes, until golden. Set aside.

3. Meanwhile, in a skillet, cook the bacon over medium heat, stirring occasionally to break up the pieces, until crispy. Using a slotted spoon, transfer the bacon to a paper towel–lined plate to drain excess fat. Very carefully remove all but 3 tablespoons of the rendered (melted) bacon fat from the skillet.

4. Add the onion to the skillet with the bacon fat and cook over medium heat until the onion is tender, 5 to 7 minutes. Add the tomatoes, vinegar, and sugar and simmer until the liquid begins to thicken, 1 to 2 minutes.

5. Place the spinach leaves in a large salad bowl and pour the hot mixture from the skillet over the top, tossing quickly to coat and wilt the spinach. Season with salt and pepper, and sprinkle in the cooked bacon and toasted pecans.

Tangy Tomato Soup

SERVES 4

What meal isn't better with a hot bowl of thick tomato soup? When you make your own, you'll be surprised at how good it is. Enjoy as part of lunch or dinner, or by itself as a snack.

2 TABLESPOONS OLIVE OIL

2 ONIONS, CHOPPED

1 TEASPOON SALT

ONE 28-OUNCE CAN WHOLE PEELED TOMATOES, WITH JUICES

3½ CUPS CHICKEN BROTH

½ CUP ORANGE JUICE

1 TEASPOON DRIED OREGANO

1 CUP CROUTONS

2 OUNCES PARMESAN CHEESE, SHAVED (SEE NOTE)

1. In a large pot, heat the oil over medium heat. Add the onions and salt and cook, stirring occasionally, until the onions are softened, 4 to 6 minutes. Add the tomatoes with their juices, the broth, orange juice, and oregano. Simmer for 10 to 15 minutes, until the soup begins to thicken.

2. Very carefully transfer the soup to a blender. Holding a kitchen towel over the lid of the blender for safety, purée the soup until it is smooth. Pour the soup into bowls and top each one with a handful of croutons and a few shavings of cheese.

Note: You can "shave" curls off a chunk of Parmesan by using a vegetable peeler. As always, make sure the piece of Parmesan is large enough to hold without putting your fingers in danger of being cut, and shave away from yourself with the peeler.

Salads and Soups

Paprika Bliss Soup

SERVES 6

Best made on a cold winter afternoon, this thick, rich soup just needs some crunchy bread on the side to make a complete meal. It will warm you inside and out.

¼ CUP (½ STICK) BUTTER

2 CUPS CHOPPED ONIONS

1 POUND FRESH MUSHROOMS, SLICED

2 TEASPOONS DRIED DILL

1 TABLESPOON PAPRIKA

1 TABLESPOON SOY SAUCE

2 CUPS CHICKEN BROTH

1 CUP MILK

3 TABLESPOONS ALL-PURPOSE FLOUR

1 TEASPOON SALT

2 TEASPOONS LEMON JUICE

¼ CUP CHOPPED FRESH PARSLEY

½ CUP SOUR CREAM

GROUND BLACK PEPPER

1. In a large pot, melt the butter over medium heat. Add the onions and sauté for 5 minutes. Add the mushrooms and sauté for 5 minutes more. Stir in the dill, paprika, soy sauce, and broth. Reduce the heat to low, cover, and simmer for 15 minutes.

2. In a small bowl, whisk the milk and flour together until well combined. Pour this into the soup, and stir thoroughly. Cover and simmer the soup, stirring occasionally, for 15 minutes more. Next, stir in the salt, lemon juice, parsley, and sour cream. Season with pepper. Reduce the heat to low and heat through (but do not boil) for 3 to 5 minutes more. Serve.

Call-It-Flower Soup

SERVES 4

Who knew cauliflower could be made into soup? Try this and see what you think. You might see this vegetable in an all-new light.

2 TABLESPOONS OLIVE OIL, PLUS MORE FOR SERVING

3 CLOVES GARLIC, SLICED

1 SMALL HEAD OF CAULIFLOWER, CHOPPED INTO FLORETS

5 CUPS CHICKEN BROTH

1 TABLESPOON DRIED THYME, PLUS MORE FOR SERVING

1 TEASPOON SALT

¼ TEASPOON GROUND BLACK PEPPER

1.   In a large pot, heat the oil over medium heat. Add the garlic and cook, stirring, until the garlic turns golden brown, 2 to 3 minutes. Use a slotted spoon to remove the garlic from the pot; set the garlic slices aside on a plate. Add the cauliflower, broth, thyme, salt, and pepper, and simmer 15 to 20 minutes.

2.   Very carefully transfer the soup to a blender. Holding a kitchen towel over the lid of the blender for safety, purée the soup until it is smooth. Scoop the soup into bowls, and top each bowl with a few pieces of the reserved garlic, a drizzle of olive oil, and a dash of thyme.

Coconut and Curry Soup

SERVES 4 TO 6

This Indian-inspired soup helps you warm up on the coldest of winter days.

2 TABLESPOONS OLIVE OIL

1½ POUNDS BONELESS, SKINLESS CHICKEN BREAST, CUT INTO 1-INCH PIECES

SALT AND GROUND BLACK PEPPER

½ CUP CHOPPED ONION

1 RED BELL PEPPER, SEEDED AND FINELY CHOPPED

2 CUPS CHICKEN BROTH

ONE 14-OUNCE CAN UNSWEETENED LIGHT COCONUT MILK

⅛ TEASPOON CAYENNE PEPPER (OR MORE, IF YOU LIKE IT SPICY!)

1 TABLESPOON BROWN SUGAR

½ TABLESPOON CURRY POWDER

JUICE OF 1 LIME

¼ CUP CHOPPED FRESH CILANTRO

COOKED RICE, FOR SERVING (OPTIONAL)

1.   In a large pot, heat the oil over medium heat. Lightly season the chicken with salt and black pepper, and carefully add it to the pot. Cook for 1 to 2 minutes, and then add the onion and bell pepper. Cook for 2 to 3 minutes more, until the vegetables start to soften.

2.   Add the broth, coconut milk, cayenne, sugar, and curry powder, and stir. Bring the soup to a simmer and cook for 10 to 15 minutes. Stir in the lime juice and cilantro, and season with salt and pepper. Serve alone as soup or over cooked rice for a heartier dish.

Slow Cooker Chowder

SERVES 6 TO 8

Slow cookers are a great way to cook. You combine all of the ingredients in the cooker, plug it in, turn it on, and then go about your other business for hours. When the bell rings, the food is hot and ready. Here is a tasty recipe using an 8-quart slow cooker. (If yours is smaller than this, adjust the ingredients accordingly.) Be sure to start the recipe well enough in advance of when you want to eat—the cooking doesn't need to be monitored, but it does go very slowly!

½ POUND BACON

5 MEDIUM POTATOES, CUT INTO ¼-INCH CUBES

8 CUPS CORN KERNELS (FRESH OR FROZEN AND THAWED)

1 MEDIUM SWEET ONION, CHOPPED

1 CUP CHOPPED CELERY

7 CLOVES GARLIC, CRUSHED

½ TEASPOON SALT, PLUS MORE AS NEEDED

4 CUPS CHICKEN STOCK

2 CUPS HEAVY CREAM

GROUND BLACK PEPPER

1.   In a large skillet, cook the bacon over medium-high heat until crispy. Transfer to a plate lined with paper towels to drain and cool. When cool enough to handle, crumble the bacon into small pieces and place them in the bowl of an 8-quart slow cooker.

2.   Add the potatoes, corn, onion, celery, garlic, salt, and stock to the slow cooker. Set the slow cooker to cook for 10 hours on low or 6 hours on high.

3.   When the time is up, carefully ladle half of the soup into a blender. Holding a kitchen towel over the lid of the blender for safety, purée the soup until it is smooth. Pour the puréed soup back into the slow cooker and stir in the cream.

4.   Allow the soup to cook, uncovered, for 15 minutes more. Season with salt and pepper, and serve.

CHAPTER SIX

Dinner for One

Chances are that you eat most of your dinners with your family or friends. Now and then, however, you will find yourself alone at home, or eating long before or after everyone else. In that case, making a dinner that serves four or more isn't effective or efficient.

The dinner recipes in this chapter are specifically designed for just one person. (The extra perk is that you can pick whatever *you* like best for the meal—no putting up with an ingredient that makes you shudder.) Remember, if you don't eat it all, you can always use the leftovers for lunch the next day.

Also keep in mind that many of the recipes in the breakfast chapter can work for dinner, especially those that make one serving, like the Mini Muffin Pizza or High-Rise Hero. You're the boss!

Tropical Ham and Cheese

SERVES 1

Dress up an old favorite with a new combo of toppings.

2 SLICES SANDWICH BREAD

2 SLICES SWISS CHEESE

2 OUNCES THINLY SLICED DELI HAM

2 THINLY SLICED PINEAPPLE ROUNDS

3 FRESH BASIL LEAVES

1 TABLESPOON BUTTER

1.   Layer one slice of bread with one slice of Swiss cheese, then the ham, pineapple, basil, and the other slice of cheese; top with the other slice of bread.

2.   In a skillet with a lid, melt the butter over medium heat. Place the sandwich in the hot butter and cover the pan. Cook until the underside of the sandwich is toasted to a golden brown, 2 to 3 minutes. Flip the sandwich and cook the other side.

3.   Remove the sandwich from the pan, let cool until you can pick it up, and enjoy!

Twisted Turkey Treat

SERVES 1

Another fun and well-known sandwich with a tangy twist on the flavor.

1 TABLESPOON GRATED PARMESAN CHEESE

2 TABLESPOONS LIGHT MAYONNAISE

2 TEASPOONS LEMON JUICE

DASH OF WORCESTERSHIRE SAUCE

SALT AND GROUND BLACK PEPPER

2 SLICES MULTIGRAIN BREAD

2 LARGE ROMAINE LETTUCE LEAVES

3 OUNCES THINLY SLICED DELI SMOKED TURKEY

2 SWEET PICKLES, THINLY SLICED IN STRIPS

In a small bowl, combine the Parmesan, mayonnaise, lemon juice, and Worcestershire sauce. Season with salt and pepper. Spread the mixture evenly on both slices of bread. Top both slices of bread with lettuce, turkey, and pickles, and then slap the two slices together.

Dinner for One

One-Pan Hamburger and Veggies

SERVES 1

Here's the perfect one-dish meal that has meat and veggies simmering together in harmony.

1 TABLESPOON OLIVE OIL

1 SMALL ONION, CHOPPED

2 STALKS CELERY, CHOPPED

2 TO 3 CARROTS, CUT INTO SMALL PIECES

⅛ TEASPOON GARLIC POWDER

⅛ TEASPOON CURRY POWDER

SALT AND GROUND BLACK PEPPER

½ POUND GROUND BEEF

1 ZUCCHINI, CUT INTO SMALL PIECES

COOKED RICE OR NOODLES, FOR SERVING (OPTIONAL)

1.   In a medium frying pan, heat the olive oil and combine the onion, celery, carrots, garlic powder, curry powder, and a little salt and pepper. Sauté over medium heat for 2 to 3 minutes.

2.   Add the beef and cook for 5 minutes more, breaking apart the meat with a wooden spoon as it cooks.

3.   Add the zucchini, cover, and cook until the veggies have softened, 5 to 8 minutes more.

4.   Serve as is or over rice or noodles for a larger meal.

Festive Fried Rice

SERVES 1

This is a nutritious—and colorful—way to dress up some leftover rice that's sitting in the refrigerator.

1 EGG

¾ CUP MIXED FROZEN PEAS, SHREDDED CARROTS, SHREDDED ZUCCHINI, AND SLICED RED BELL PEPPER

½ CUP COOKED BROWN RICE (LEFT OVER FROM ANOTHER MEAL)

1 TABLESPOON WATER

⅛ TEASPOON SOY SAUCE

⅛ TEASPOON GARLIC POWDER

⅛ TEASPOON GROUND GINGER

1. Crack the egg into a small bowl, beat with a fork, and set aside.

2. In a small frying pan, cook the mixed vegetables over medium heat. As the veggies begin to soften, add the rice and water. Cover and cook for 2 minutes; then add the beaten egg. Stir the ingredients together and cook until the egg is cooked through, 3 to 4 minutes. Add the soy sauce, garlic powder, and ginger, and stir until combined.

Spaghetti for Singles

SERVES 1

Making spaghetti usually yields far too much for one person. Try this version instead. Fancy—and just right for one.

BUTTER, FOR THE PAN
8 CHERRY TOMATOES, HALVED
1 SMALL CLOVE GARLIC, WHOLE AND UNPEELED
½ TEASPOON SUGAR
1 TEASPOON BALSAMIC VINEGAR
1 TEASPOON OLIVE OIL
SALT
3.5 OUNCES SPAGHETTI NOODLES (ABOUT A LARGE FISTFUL)
1 TABLESPOON GRATED PARMESAN CHEESE

1. Preheat the oven to 375°F.

2. Lightly butter a small ovenproof dish, and put the tomato halves and garlic in it.

3. In a small bowl, combine the sugar, vinegar, and oil. Drizzle this over the tomatoes. Roast the tomatoes for 25 to 30 minutes.

4. Meanwhile, bring a medium saucepan of salted water to a boil. Add the spaghetti to the boiling water and cook as directed on the package, usually 8 to 12 minutes, until al dente. Carefully remove from the heat and drain the spaghetti into a colander.

5. Pour the spaghetti into a serving bowl. Add the roasted tomatoes and toss; discard the garlic or squeeze out the roasted garlic clove from the skin, mash it, and mix it into the spaghetti. Sprinkle Parmesan on top.

Stuffed Zukes

SERVES 2

One half of these stuffed zukes is usually enough for one person—but what is the point of making only half a zucchini? Make the other one at the same time in case you're hungrier than you thought, or you want to share with a friend.

1 CUP UNCOOKED WILD RICE

SALT

1 TABLESPOON OLIVE OIL, PLUS MORE FOR BRUSHING

1 MEDIUM ZUCCHINI, HALVED LENGTHWISE

GROUND BLACK PEPPER

¼ CUP CHOPPED ONION

½ CLOVE GARLIC, MINCED

½ TABLESPOON CHOPPED FRESH DILL

⅓ CUP GRATED SHARP CHEDDAR CHEESE

1. Preheat the oven to 375°F.

2. Place the rice in a large bowl, add enough cool water to cover, and soak for 10 minutes. Drain and rinse the rice and place it in a large pot. Add enough water to cover, a pinch of salt, and the olive oil, and bring to boil. Reduce the heat to low, cover, and simmer until just tender, 35 to 40 minutes. Set aside to cool.

3. Meanwhile, scoop out the flesh and seeds of the zucchini halves to create a bowl in which to stuff all of your ingredients. Save the insides!

4. Brush the exterior of the zucchini halves completely with olive oil, and then sprinkle them with salt and pepper. Place the zucchini cut-side up in a baking dish with a lid.

5. Chop up the reserved zucchini insides, place them in a large bowl, and add the onion, garlic, and dill. Mix well. Add the cooked wild rice and half of the cheese, and mix well. Mound the mixture in each zucchini shell, using as much as possible without the shells overflowing, and bake, covered, for 25 minutes.

6. Remove the baking dish, sprinkle the rest of the cheese on top of the zucchini filling, and bake, uncovered, for 10 minutes more, until the cheese has melted. Allow to cool for a few minutes before eating—it will be hot!

Slow Cooker Chicken

SERVES 1, WITH LEFTOVERS

It's hard to believe anything this good can be this easy, so find out for yourself. This recipe makes quite a bit of food, so you'll definitely have leftovers for lunch—lucky you!

4 FROZEN BONELESS, SKINLESS CHICKEN BREAST HALVES
ONE 15.5-OUNCE CAN BLACK BEANS, DRAINED
ONE 15.5-OUNCE CAN CORN, DRAINED
ONE 15-OUNCE JAR SALSA
4 OUNCES (½ PACKAGE) FAT-FREE CREAM CHEESE

Place all of the ingredients *except* for the cream cheese in the slow cooker (yes, the chicken breasts really do go in FROZEN). Cook on high for 4 to 5 hours. Then add the cream cheese, stirring it in so it melts, and let the dish sit for 30 minutes before eating.

Foiled Again Chicken

SERVES 1

This is fun, simple, and tasty—and good for you. Better yet, it can be whipped up within an hour.

1 BONELESS, SKINLESS CHICKEN BREAST
10 BABY CARROTS, HALVED
½ CUP CHOPPED CELERY
½ CUP DICED RAW POTATO
1 TABLESPOON OLIVE OIL
GARLIC SALT
GROUND BLACK PEPPER
POULTRY SEASONING

1.   Preheat the oven to 350°F.

2.   Pull out a sheet of aluminum foil approximately the size of a cereal box. Place the chicken breast in the center of the foil. Divide the chopped veggies equally and set half on either side of the chicken. Pour the olive oil over everything, and season with garlic salt, pepper, and poultry seasoning to taste. Fold the sides of the foil over to form a pouch, but do not poke any holes in it. Place the pouch on a baking sheet and bake for 1 hour. Open carefully when ready to eat—the steam will be very hot.

73

Dinner for One

White Angel Hair

A rich meal just for one! Add garlic bread and/or a salad to make it more complete.

SALT

2 OUNCES UNCOOKED ANGEL HAIR PASTA

2 TABLESPOONS BUTTER

3 TABLESPOONS CHOPPED SWEET ONION

1 CLOVE GARLIC, MINCED

⅔ CUP HEAVY CREAM

¼ CUP GRATED PARMESAN CHEESE

¼ CUP CHOPPED FRESH BASIL

GROUND BLACK PEPPER

1.   Bring a large pot of lightly salted water to a boil. Add the pasta to the boiling water and cook as directed on the package, until al dente.

2.   Meanwhile, in a saucepan, melt the butter over medium heat. Stir in the onion and cook for 3 minutes; then stir in the garlic and continue cooking until the onion is translucent, 1 to 2 minutes. Pour in the heavy cream and stir in the Parmesan cheese and basil. Season with salt and pepper. Bring to a simmer; then reduce the heat to medium-low and simmer for 2 minutes.

3.   When the pasta is done, carefully set aside ½ cup of the hot cooking water, and then drain the pasta into a colander. If the cream sauce is too thick, use the reserved pasta water to thin it.

4.   Transfer the pasta to a bowl, pour the sauce over the top, and serve.

Southwestern Salad

SERVES 1

Combine your love of Mexican food with the good nutrition of a salad in this dish.

½ RIPE AVOCADO
¾ CUP PACKED FRESH CILANTRO
½ CUP PLAIN NONFAT YOGURT
2 SCALLIONS, CHOPPED
1 CLOVE GARLIC, QUARTERED
1 TABLESPOON LIME JUICE
½ TEASPOON SUGAR
½ TEASPOON SALT
3 CUPS MIXED GREENS
½ CUP RINSED CANNED BLACK BEANS
½ CUP FRESH CORN KERNELS
½ CUP GRAPE TOMATOES

1.   In an unplugged blender, combine the avocado, cilantro, yogurt, scallions, garlic, lime juice, sugar, and salt; plug in the blender and blend until smooth.

2.   Place the greens in a salad bowl; toss with 2 tablespoons of the avocado dressing. (Refrigerate the rest for next time—or use it for tortillas!) Top the greens with black beans, corn, and tomatoes.

Bacon and Cheese Risotto

SERVES 1

This creamy, delicious rice can be served as a side dish, but works well by itself as a meal. It takes a while to cook, so start making it before you're super hungry!

4 SLICES BACON
1 LARGE ONION, DICED
½ CUP UNCOOKED ARBORIO RICE
2 TEASPOONS RUBBED SAGE (SEE NOTE)
3 CUPS WATER, PLUS MORE AS NEEDED
¼ TEASPOON SALT
GROUND BLACK PEPPER
1 CUP FROZEN PEAS
1 CUP GOAT CHEESE

1.   Place a medium skillet over medium-high heat. Add the bacon and cook until it is crispy, about 10 minutes. Transfer the bacon to a paper towel–lined plate to drain. Add the onion to the bacon fat left in the skillet and cook, stirring occasionally, for 5 minutes. Add the rice and sage and cook, stirring continuously, for about 2 minutes. Add the water and salt; then season with pepper and stir.

2.   Reduce the heat to medium and simmer, stirring occasionally, until the rice is just cooked, 30 to 40 minutes.

3.   Add the peas and a couple of tablespoons of water, if the pan looks dry. Stir in the goat cheese. Chop the cooked bacon and add it to the risotto. Cook until the cheese is melted and the peas are hot.

Note: Rubbed sage is dried sage leaves that have been crushed (not ground). Look for it in the spice aisle of your supermarket. And be sure not to confuse it with *ground* sage! Even though it sounds like the same thing, ground herbs and spices pack a greater flavor punch than their whole or crushed counterparts, which isn't always what you're looking for.

Gourmet Chicken Skillet

SERVES 1

Chicken and asparagus get jazzed up in this deluxe, protein-rich dish.

3 TABLESPOONS BUTTER

2 TABLESPOONS OLIVE OIL

½ TEASPOON DRIED PARSLEY

½ TEASPOON DRIED BASIL

⅛ TEASPOON DRIED OREGANO

1½ CLOVES GARLIC, MINCED

¼ TEASPOON SALT

1½ TEASPOONS LEMON JUICE

2 BONELESS, SKINLESS CHICKEN BREAST HALVES, CUT INTO SLICES

½ POUND FRESH ASPARAGUS, TRIMMED AND CUT INTO THIRDS

1 CUP SLICED FRESH MUSHROOMS

1.   In a skillet, melt the butter with the oil over medium-high heat. Stir in the parsley, basil, oregano, garlic, salt, and lemon juice. Add the chicken and cook, stirring, until it is browned, about 3 minutes. Reduce the heat to medium and cook, stirring, until the chicken is cooked through (no longer pink inside), about 10 minutes more.

2.   Next, add the asparagus and cook until it is bright green and just starting to become tender, about 3 minutes. Stir in the mushrooms and cook for 3 minutes more. Serve hot.

Creamy Corn and Ham

SERVES 1

This is good "home cooking" and great comfort food.

¼ CUP UNCOOKED RICE

¼ CUP CHOPPED ONION

¾ CUP WATER

4.5 OUNCES CREAMED CORN

¼ CUP DICED HAM

2 TABLESPOONS LIGHT CREAM

2 TABLESPOONS GRATED CHEDDAR CHEESE

1.   In a medium saucepan, combine the rice, onion, and water and bring to a boil over high heat, stirring occasionally. Reduce the heat to maintain a simmer and cook for 10 to 12 minutes more, until all of the liquid has been absorbed.

2.   Stir in the creamed corn, ham, and cream and simmer until the mixture is heated through.

3.   Spoon the mixture into a microwave-safe serving dish, top with the cheese, and heat in the microwave until the cheese has melted.

Ocean 'Dilla

SERVES 1

Quesadillas are fun and quick to make. Adding fish is just another way to enjoy them and be healthy, too.

ONE 5-OUNCE CAN TUNA PACKED IN OIL OR WATER, DRAINED
2 TABLESPOONS MAYONNAISE
1 TABLESPOON CHOPPED CELERY
2 TORTILLAS
4 SLICES AVOCADO
2 TABLESPOONS GRATED MONTEREY JACK CHEESE
½ CUP SALSA, FOR DIPPING

Place the tuna in a small bowl. Mix in the mayonnaise and celery. Spread the tuna mixture on a tortilla and top with the avocado slices, then the cheese. Top with the second tortilla, place the "sandwich" on a microwave-safe plate, and microwave on high for 30 to 60 seconds. Cut into four pieces and serve with the salsa for dipping.

Leeky Chicken

SERVES 1

Never had a leek before? If you like onions, you will like leeks. This is a great recipe for any chicken you have left over from the night before.

½ CUP UNCOOKED MACARONI PASTA
½ TEASPOON OLIVE OIL
½ SMALL LEEK, SLICED THIN (SEE NOTE)
1 CUP MIXED FROZEN PEAS AND CORN
½ CUP SHREDDED SKINLESS COOKED CHICKEN
1 TEASPOON ALL-PURPOSE FLOUR
⅓ CUP EVAPORATED LIGHT MILK
2 TABLESPOONS CHEDDAR CHEESE
FRESH PARSLEY OR OREGANO, CHOPPED

1. Preheat the oven to 375°F.

2. Bring a large pot of lightly salted water to a boil. Add the pasta to the boiling water and cook as directed on the package, until al dente. Drain the pasta in a colander and set aside.

3. In a skillet, heat the oil over medium heat. Add the leek and cook for 5 minutes. Add the mixed vegetables and chicken and cook for 4 minutes more. Next, add the flour and stir to combine. Add the milk and simmer for 2 minutes, until thoroughly warmed. Finally, add the cooked pasta and toss it to coat the noodles.

4. Transfer the mixture to a baking dish. Sprinkle with the cheese, and bake for 15 minutes, until the cheese is melted and golden brown. Sprinkle with parsley or oregano and serve.

Note: Leeks are a member of the onion family that grow in sandy soil. As a result, there can often be grit or sand between the leek's layers, so it's important to wash leeks carefully. One good way to do this is: Fill a large bowl with water and set a colander in the bowl (the water should come up through the colander). Rinse off the outside of the leek and trim it; then slice it in desired-size pieces. Place the leek pieces in the colander and swish them around in the water to loosen any grit; then let them stand for 10 minutes or so. Carefully lift the colander out of the water—you'll probably notice lots of grit on the bottom of the bowl of water, but at least it's not on your leeks anymore! Give the leeks in the colander a final rinse under cool, running water and let them drain before using them.

CHAPTER SEVEN

Dinner for Everyone

Ah, dinnertime! It can be the most fun meal of the day. You're not hurrying to get to school, like at breakfast. You're not on the run from one place to the next, like at lunch. Snack time was long ago—and now your homework is done, and it's time to relax and enjoy good food with your family.

What can you make? This chapter offers a variety of options. Try a bunch and see which ones you like the most.

Tasty Lasagna

SERVES 8

That famous cartoon cat Garfield is a huge fan of lasagna—and this recipe is so good, you'll understand why! You can use store-bought pasta sauce or make your own with the recipe on the next page. Yes, it's extra work on an already long recipe, but it'll be worth every minute when you take that first bite.

9 LASAGNA NOODLES

1 TABLESPOON OLIVE OIL

8 OUNCES ITALIAN SAUSAGE

15 OUNCES RICOTTA CHEESE

1½ CUPS GRATED MOZZARELLA CHEESE

¼ CUP GRATED PARMESAN CHEESE

SALT AND GROUND BLACK PEPPER

6 CUPS PASTA SAUCE, HOMEMADE (SEE SAUCE IT UP! RECIPE, ON THE NEXT PAGE)
    OR STORE-BOUGHT

1.   Preheat the oven to 350°F. Line a baking sheet with paper towels.

2.   Bring a large pot of lightly salted water to a boil. Add the lasagna noodles to the boiling water and cook as directed on the package, until al dente. Drain the noodles in a colander and rinse them with cold water. Lay the noodles on the lined baking sheet and pat them dry with additional paper towels.

3.   In a skillet, heat the oil over medium-high heat. Add the sausage and cook for 5 to 7 minutes. Make sure to break up the sausage with a wooden spoon so the meat is crumbly and cooked through. Transfer the sausage to a bowl and set aside.

4.   In a large bowl, combine the ricotta, 1 cup of the mozzarella, and the Parmesan. Season with salt and pepper. Divide the cheese mixture evenly among the noodles, spreading it in a layer over each noodle.

5.   In a 13-by-9-inch baking dish, spoon in enough sauce to thinly cover the bottom. Lay three noodles lengthwise over the sauce, with the cheese-side up. Sprinkle half of the sausage over the top and then add more sauce. Top with three more noodles (cheese-side up), the remaining sausage, and then more sauce. Put the last three noodles on the top and cover with the remaining sauce. Sprinkle the remaining ½ cup mozzarella on top.

6.   Cover the baking dish with foil and bake for 45 minutes. Serve hot!

Sauce It Up!

1 TABLESPOON OLIVE OIL
½ CUP CHOPPED ONION
2 CLOVES GARLIC, MINCED
ONE 14.5-OUNCE CAN DICED TOMATOES, WITH JUICES
ONE 28-OUNCE CAN CRUSHED TOMATOES
ONE 6-OUNCE CAN TOMATO PASTE
1 TABLESPOON DRIED BASIL

In a medium saucepan, heat the oil over medium-high heat. Add the onion and garlic and cook until the onion starts to brown, about 4 minutes. Add the tomatoes, tomato paste, and basil and stir well. Bring the mixture to a boil, and then reduce the heat to low. Cover and simmer for 30 minutes, stirring occasionally.

Ramen Upgrade

SERVES 4 TO 6

If you've ever had to stay up late studying, you've probably made ramen. It's quick, easy, and inexpensive. Here's a way to use the package to make something a little fancier.

1 TABLESPOON SESAME OIL

1 POUND BONELESS, SKINLESS CHICKEN BREAST, CUT INTO THIN SLICES

ONE 1-POUND BAG FROZEN ASIAN-STYLE MIXED VEGETABLES

ONE 3-OUNCE PACKAGE CHICKEN-FLAVOR RAMEN NOODLES

2 TABLESPOONS SOY SAUCE

1 CLOVE GARLIC, MINCED

1 TEASPOON GROUND GINGER

¼ CUP WATER

1.   In a skillet, heat the oil over medium-high heat. Add the chicken and cook, stirring often, until it is no longer pink. Add the vegetables and cook, covered, for 5 minutes more, until the vegetables are cooked through.

2.   Meanwhile, bring a medium pot of water to a boil. Cook the ramen noodles (minus the flavor packet) according to the directions on the package. Drain the noodles in a colander.

3.   In a small bowl, combine the soy sauce, garlic, ginger, ramen flavor packet, and water. Mix well and pour over the chicken and vegetables. Add the noodles, toss to coat, and serve.

"Grilled" Joes

SERVES 4

Who doesn't like sloppy joes? They're messy and delicious! This is a fresh spin on the usual sandwich.

1 TABLESPOON OLIVE OIL

1 POUND GROUND BEEF

½ CUP CHOPPED ONION

1 CLOVE GARLIC, FINELY CHOPPED

1 TEASPOON SWEET PAPRIKA

½ TEASPOON LIQUID SMOKE (SEE NOTE)

1 CUP KETCHUP

1 TABLESPOON BALSAMIC VINEGAR

1 TABLESPOON WORCESTERSHIRE SAUCE

3 TABLESPOONS BROWN SUGAR

SALT

4 HOAGIE BUNS, SPLIT

In a large skillet, heat the olive oil and sauté the beef, onion, and garlic over high heat until the beef is browned and all of the liquid in the pan has evaporated, about 10 minutes. Reduce the heat to low, add the paprika and liquid smoke, and stir thoroughly. Stir in the ketchup, vinegar, Worcestershire sauce, and sugar, and season with salt. Cover and simmer, stirring often so nothing burns, for 30 minutes. Divide the mixture evenly among the hoagie buns and serve.

Note: Liquid smoke is a seasoning that adds a "smoky" flavor to foods, like the flavor you'd get by cooking something over a fragrant wood fire. It is available at many grocery stores—check near the barbecue sauces.

Tamale Temptation

SERVES 4 TO 6

One-dish meals are wonderful (and require less cleanup!), and this one is inexpensive to make. This recipe makes good use of what you may already have in the cupboard.

3 TABLESPOONS OLIVE OIL

1 SMALL ONION, CHOPPED

1 LARGE CLOVE GARLIC, FINELY CHOPPED

1 POUND GROUND BEEF

1¼ TEASPOONS SALT

1 TEASPOON PLUS 1 TABLESPOON SUGAR

2 TABLESPOONS WHITE VINEGAR

ONE 8-OUNCE CAN TOMATO SAUCE

ONE 15-OUNCE CAN PINTO BEANS

2 CUPS FROZEN CORN, THAWED

⅓ CUP ALL-PURPOSE FLOUR

⅔ CUP CORNMEAL

1 TEASPOON BAKING POWDER

1 EGG

½ CUP BUTTERMILK

1 CUP GRATED CHEDDAR CHEESE

1.   Preheat the oven to 400°F.

2.   In a 12-inch ovenproof skillet, heat 1 tablespoon of the oil over medium heat. Add the onions and sauté until they are translucent, about 7 to 8 minutes. Add the garlic and sauté for 1 minute more. Raise the heat to medium-high and add the ground beef. Cook, breaking up the meat with a wooden spoon, until the beef is browned and crumbly. Stir in ¾ teaspoon of the salt, 1 teaspoon of the sugar, the vinegar, tomato sauce, beans, and corn. Simmer for a few minutes.

3.   In a large bowl, whisk together the flour, cornmeal, baking powder, remaining ½ teaspoon salt, and remaining 1 tablespoon sugar. In another bowl, whisk together the egg, buttermilk, and remaining 2 tablespoons oil.

4.   Pour the liquid mixture into the dry mixture and stir well to combine. Next, stir in ½ cup of the cheese. Pour this over the beef mixture in the skillet—do not stir. Top with the remaining ½ cup cheese and place the pan in the oven. Bake for 20 minutes, until the cornbread top is golden brown.

Upside-Down Biscuit Pizza

SERVES 5

This recipe is one of the quickest, simplest dinners you can possibly make (you even get to cheat a little on the crust).

1½ POUNDS GROUND BEEF
ONE 15-OUNCE CAN TOMATO SAUCE
1½ CUPS SHREDDED MOZZARELLA CHEESE
ONE 10-OUNCE PACKAGE REFRIGERATED BISCUITS (10 BISCUITS)

1. Preheat the oven to 400°F.

2. In a skillet, cook the beef over medium heat, breaking it up with a wooden spoon as it cooks, until thoroughly browned. Carefully drain off the fat from the pan, and then stir in the tomato sauce and cook for a minute or two to heat through. Transfer the mixture to a 13-by-9-inch baking dish, and sprinkle with the cheese.

3. On your countertop, flatten the biscuits with your hand, and then arrange them on top of the cheese in a single layer. Bake for 15 minutes or until the biscuits are golden brown.

Simple Shepherd's Pie

SERVES 4

Shepherd's pie is a well-known dish throughout the world. It can be tricky to make, but this recipe makes it much simpler, if you happen to have some leftover mashed potatoes—or a package of them.

OIL OR BUTTER, FOR THE PAN

1 POUND GROUND BEEF

2 CUPS MIXED FROZEN VEGETABLES

ONE 10.75-OUNCE CAN CONDENSED TOMATO SOUP

½ CUP BEEF BROTH

1 TABLESPOON WORCESTERSHIRE SAUCE

1 TEASPOON DRIED MINCED ONION

½ TEASPOON DRIED THYME

⅛ TEASPOON GROUND BLACK PEPPER

ONE 24-OUNCE PACKAGE REFRIGERATED PREPARED MASHED POTATOES

½ CUP SHREDDED CHEDDAR CHEESE

1.   Preheat the oven to 375°F. Lightly grease an 8-inch-square baking dish with oil or butter.

2.   In a skillet, cook the ground beef over medium heat until it is browned. Carefully drain off the fat from the pan, and then stir in the mixed vegetables, tomato soup, broth, Worcestershire sauce, dried onion, thyme, and pepper. Bring the mixture to a boil, stirring frequently, and then transfer to the prepared baking dish.

3.   Place the potatoes in a large bowl and stir until smooth. Spoon the potatoes into mounds on top of the meat mixture. Bake, uncovered, for 20 to 25 minutes, or until heated through and bubbly. Sprinkle with the cheese and let stand for 10 minutes before serving.

Ham Cass

This essentially one-step recipe (put everything in a dish and bake it) seems almost too good to be true, but it isn't. Try it!

1½ CUPS MILK

ONE 10.75-OUNCE CAN CONDENSED CREAM OF CELERY SOUP

2 CUPS DICED COOKED HAM

1 CUP UNCOOKED MACARONI PASTA

ONE 4-OUNCE CAN SLICED MUSHROOMS, DRAINED

2 TABLESPOONS DICED PIMENTO PEPPER

½ CUP CHOPPED ONION

½ CUP SHREDDED CHEDDAR CHEESE (OR YOUR FAVORITE GRATED CHEESE)

1. Preheat the oven to 375°F.

2. In a casserole dish, slowly stir the milk into the soup. Next, stir in the ham, macaroni, mushrooms, pimento, and onion. Bake, covered, for 40 minutes, until the macaroni is tender. Sprinkle the top evenly with the cheese and bake, uncovered, for 10 minutes more. Let stand for a few minutes before serving.

Cheeseburger Casserole

SERVES 4 TO 6

This tastes like a juicy cheeseburger, without the bun. Add a loaf of hot French bread if you need a little something to go with it.

1 TABLESPOON OLIVE OIL, PLUS MORE FOR THE PAN
SALT
3 CUPS UNCOOKED WIDE EGG NOODLES
1½ CUPS SOUR CREAM
½ CUP GRATED PARMESAN CHEESE
¾ POUND GROUND BEEF
1 RED BELL PEPPER, SEEDED AND CHOPPED
½ CUP MINCED ONION
1 TABLESPOON TOMATO PASTE
1 TEASPOON ITALIAN SEASONING
ONE 14-OUNCE CAN DICED TOMATOES, WITH JUICES
2 CUPS GRATED CHEDDAR CHEESE (OR YOUR FAVORITE GRATED CHEESE)

1. Preheat the oven to 425°F. Grease a 13-by-9-inch baking dish with oil.

2. Bring a large pot of salted water to a boil. Add the noodles and cook according to the package directions. Drain the noodles in a colander and put them in the prepared baking dish. Toss with the sour cream, Parmesan, and a little salt.

3. In a skillet, heat the oil over medium-high heat. Add the ground beef and cook, breaking it up with a wooden spoon as it cooks, until thoroughly browned, about 4 minutes. Add the bell pepper and onion and cook, about 3 minutes. Add the tomato paste, Italian seasoning, and a little salt, and stir. Add the tomatoes and their juices and bring to a simmer. Cook, stirring occasionally, for 2 to 3 minutes.

4. Pour the beef mixture over the noodles and sprinkle with the cheddar. Bake for 15 to 20 minutes, until the cheese has melted.

Sweet Spiced Pork Chops

SERVES 4

Cinnamon and apple may make you think of dessert, but this time you can find them in a main dish. Serve with some steamed green beans or other vegetable you have on hand.

2 TABLESPOONS BUTTER

4 BONELESS PORK CHOPS

3 TABLESPOONS BROWN SUGAR

1 TEASPOON GROUND CINNAMON

½ TEASPOON GROUND OR FRESHLY GRATED NUTMEG

¼ TEASPOON SALT

4 MEDIUM TART APPLES, CORED AND THINLY SLICED

2 TABLESPOONS CHOPPED PECANS

1.   In a skillet, melt 1 tablespoon of the butter over medium heat. Add the pork chops and cook for 4 to 5 minutes on each side.

2.   Meanwhile, in a small bowl, combine the brown sugar, cinnamon, nutmeg, and salt.

3.   Transfer the pork chops to a plate and cover them with foil to keep them warm. Set aside.

4.   In the same skillet, combine the apples, pecans, remaining 1 tablespoon butter, and the brown sugar mixture. Cook over low heat until the apples are tender, about 10 minutes. Scoop the mixture on top of the pork chops and serve.

Deep-Dish Spaghetti Pizza

SERVES 6 TO 8

How can pizza and spaghetti be in the same dish? Like this!

BUTTER, FOR THE PAN
½ TEASPOON SALT
12 OUNCES UNCOOKED SPAGHETTI
1 POUND SWEET PORK SAUSAGE
2 OUNCES PEPPERONI SLICES
ONE 26-OUNCE JAR TOMATO AND BASIL PASTA SAUCE
¼ CUP GRATED PARMESAN CHEESE
8 OUNCES SHREDDED ITALIAN THREE-CHEESE BLEND

1.   Preheat the oven to 350°F. Lightly grease a 13-by-9-inch baking dish with butter.

2.   Bring a large pot of salted water to a boil. Add the spaghetti to the boiling water and cook according to the package directions, until al dente. Drain the pasta in a colander and then add it to the prepared baking dish. Set aside.

3.   In a large skillet, cook the sausage over medium-high heat, stirring occasionally, for 5 minutes, until browned. Using a slotted spoon, transfer the browned sausage to the dish with the pasta.

4.   Put the pepperoni in the skillet and cook over medium-high heat until slightly crisp, about 4 minutes.

5.   Pour the pasta sauce over the pasta and sausage. Arrange half of the pepperoni slices across the sauce. Sprinkle evenly with the cheeses and layer the remaining pepperoni slices on top. Cover the dish with aluminum foil and bake for 30 minutes. Remove the foil and bake for 10 minutes more, until the cheese has melted and begins to brown.

Cheesy Slow-Cooking Stew

SERVES 4 TO 6

Here is a recipe that's slow-cooked in a slow cooker, so put it together, turn it on, and go away! Come back and it's done.

6 BRATWURST LINKS

4 MEDIUM POTATOES, PEELED AND CUBED

½ CUP MINCED ONION

ONE 15-OUNCE CAN GREEN BEANS, DRAINED

1 SMALL RED BELL PEPPER, SEEDED AND CHOPPED

2 CUPS SHREDDED CHEDDAR CHEESE

ONE 10.75-OUNCE CAN CREAM OF MUSHROOM SOUP

⅔ CUP WATER

1. In a large skillet, cook the brats over medium heat until browned. Remove from the skillet and let cool slightly—when cool enough to handle, cut the brats crosswise into ½-inch slices.

2. Place the sliced brats in the slow cooker, add the remaining ingredients, stir, and cook on medium for 3 hours. That's it!

Rosemary Roasts

SERVES 4

This full, rich dinner will be a hit with your family year-round.

6 TABLESPOONS OLIVE OIL, PLUS MORE FOR THE PAN
1 POUND BRATWURST LINKS, CUT CROSSWISE INTO ½-INCH SLICES
2½ POUNDS CHICKEN PIECES (BREASTS, THIGHS, DRUMSTICKS, ETC.)
PINCH OF SALT
2 POUNDS POTATOES, CUT INTO 1-INCH CHUNKS
2½ TABLESPOONS CHOPPED FRESH ROSEMARY LEAVES
1 TEASPOON RED WINE VINEGAR

1.   Preheat the oven to 450°F. Grease a large baking dish with oil.

2.   In a large skillet, heat 1 tablespoon of the oil over medium heat. Add the brat slices and cook until browned on both sides, about 5 minutes. Transfer the brats to the prepared baking dish and set aside.

3.   Add 3 tablespoons of the oil to the skillet and return it to the heat. Add the chicken pieces, season them with salt, and cook for 7 to 10 minutes. Transfer to the baking dish with the brats and set aside.

4.   Add the potatoes to the skillet and cook until lightly browned. Transfer to the baking dish with the chicken and brats.

5.   Drizzle the potatoes, chicken, and brats with the remaining 2 tablespoons olive oil and sprinkle with half of the rosemary. Bake for 15 minutes. Turn each piece of chicken over, and stir the potatoes and sausage. Add the remaining rosemary and the red wine vinegar, and bake for 15 minutes more. Serve each person some of the potatoes, a piece or two of chicken, and some of the brats, and drizzle with any of the juices left in the pan.

Autumn Chili

SERVES 4

Nothing says autumn more than pumpkin, turkey, and chili. This recipe blends all three of them together.

1 TABLESPOON OLIVE OIL

1 CUP CHOPPED ONION

½ CUP CHOPPED GREEN BELL PEPPER

½ CUP CHOPPED YELLOW BELL PEPPER

1 CLOVE GARLIC, MINCED

1 POUND GROUND TURKEY

ONE 14.5-OUNCE CAN DICED TOMATOES, JUICES DRAINED

2 CUPS PUMPKIN PURÉE (SEE NOTE, PAGE 28)

1½ TABLESPOONS CHILI POWDER

½ TEASPOON GROUND BLACK PEPPER

SALT

½ CUP SHREDDED CHEDDAR CHEESE (OR YOUR FAVORITE SHREDDED CHEESE)

½ CUP SOUR CREAM

1. In a large skillet, heat the oil over medium heat. Add the onion, bell peppers, and garlic and sauté until tender. Stir in the turkey and cook, breaking it up with a wooden spoon, until evenly browned. Stir in the tomatoes and pumpkin. Add the chili powder and black pepper, and season with salt.

2. Reduce the heat to low, cover, and simmer for 20 minutes. Top with the cheese and sour cream, and serve.

Potato Party

SERVINGS WILL VARY

Uh-oh! A dozen people are coming to your house and you're in charge of feeding them? What do they like? Is anyone a vegetarian? What if they're all really picky? Don't panic. This meal (and the next recipe, Burrito Bonanza, page 101) is designed to make sure everyone goes home happy—and full.

This recipe doesn't have specific amounts of ingredients because it's up to you to tailor it to the crowd coming to your house. The meal is based on one large baked potato per person. If you're using smaller potatoes, increase the number. (If your group is a lot of little people, you might prepare small taters intentionally.) If your group is a bunch of hungry teenagers, it might just be best to see how many potatoes your oven can fit at one time.

Line up toppings in bowls or other containers on your table or countertop, and let people top their potatoes with whatever they like. Remember to put spoons in the topping containers! The more options you give your guests, the happier they will be, so think creatively. Butter and sour cream are great, but not too imaginative. Try some of the ideas here—you're sure to find a new family favorite. Some toppings will require preparation ahead of time—these are marked with an asterisk.

EXTRA-LARGE BAKING POTATOES
OLIVE OIL OR BUTTER

OPTIONAL TOPPINGS:
CRISPY COOKED BACON*
SOUR CREAM
BUTTER
GRATED CHEESE*
STEAMED BROCCOLI*
SALSA
CHILI
CHOPPED CHIVES*
BARBECUE OR PASTA SAUCE
RANCH DRESSING
GUACAMOLE*
GRILLED MUSHROOMS AND ONIONS*
SALT AND GROUND BLACK PEPPER
DRIED BASIL, CILANTRO, OREGANO, OR DILL

continued ▶

Potato Party *continued*

1. Preheat the oven to 350°F.

2. Rub the outside skin of the potatoes with olive oil or butter to keep them soft as they bake. Poke each potato in four different spots with a fork. (This allows the steam to escape as they bake—and prevents potato explosions in the oven, which can be a real mess!) Place the potatoes in the oven and bake for 45 minutes. Test them for doneness: They are done when you can stick a fork into them and they are soft. If they still feel too firm, keep baking for 5 to 10 minutes more and test them again.

3. While the potatoes are baking, prepare any toppings you want to serve.

4. When it's time to eat, place each potato in a deep dish or bowl (those toppings spill over!), split the tops, and hand them out to your guests so they can design their own dinner.

The Cookbook for Teens

Burrito Bonanza

SERVINGS WILL VARY

This meal is based on the same idea as the Potato Party (see page 99). Instead of designing your own potato, this one allows you to design your own burrito.

Depending on the age and appetite of your guests, plan on at least two burritos per person if using large 10-inch tortillas; four burritos per person if you're using smaller tortillas.

You provide a pile of warmed-up tortillas and bowls of toppings (remember the spoons!). Then let the burrito building begin! Some toppings will require preparation ahead of time—these are marked with an asterisk.

OIL, FOR WARMING THE TORTILLAS
CORN AND/OR FLOUR TORTILLAS
CHIPS, FOR SCOOPING UP WAYWARD TOPPINGS

OPTIONAL TOPPINGS:
REFRIED BEANS
BLACK BEANS
SOUR CREAM
SALSA
GUACAMOLE*
GRATED CHEESE*
PEPPERS (RED OR GREEN BELL, OR HOT)
GRILLED MUSHROOMS AND ONIONS*
COOKED GROUND BEEF OR TURKEY*
GRILLED CHICKEN*
COOKED RICE*
COOKED CORN KERNELS
LETTUCE
TOMATOES

1. In a skillet, heat a little oil over medium heat and warm the tortillas one at a time, cooking them for a minute or so on each side. (Yes, you could just microwave a stack of tortillas, but the skillet gives them a better taste!) As they are done, slide them onto plates for guests to start building their burritos.

2. Hand around a bag of chips for people to scoop up whatever falls out of the burritos!

CHAPTER EIGHT

Dessert

Like a teenage character on a popular sitcom once said, "There is full . . . and then there is *dessert*-full." In other words, no matter how much you might have eaten for dinner, there's always room for dessert! These yummy recipes will make you glad you didn't completely fill up on your meal.

Muffin Mania

MAKES 12 MUFFINS

Muffins make a tasty treat any time of the day—they can even be a great dessert. You'll agree when you sink your teeth into these apple-cinnamon delights.

¼ TABLESPOON OLIVE OIL, FOR THE PAN

2 EGGS

7 TABLESPOONS BUTTER

½ CUP SUGAR

½ CUP ALL-PURPOSE FLOUR

1 TEASPOON BAKING POWDER

¼ CUP MAPLE SYRUP

1 LARGE COOKING APPLE, SUCH AS ROME OR GALA, PEELED,
    QUARTERED, AND CORED

LARGE PINCH OF GROUND CINNAMON

1.   Preheat the oven to 400°F. Grease a 12-cup muffin pan with the oil.

2.   Crack the eggs into a small bowl and whisk them.

3.   In a large bowl, using a hand mixer, or in the bowl of a stand mixer fitted with the paddle attachment, beat the butter and sugar together until smooth and combined. Add half of the whisked eggs to the butter mixture and beat well. Using a sieve or flour sifter, sift half of the flour into the batter and mix again. Add the baking powder and remaining egg, and sift the other half of the flour into the batter; mix thoroughly. Add the syrup and mix one more time.

4.   Finely chop the apple and add it to the batter along with the cinnamon. Stir to combine.

5.   Using a spoon, fill each muffin cup three-quarters full of batter. Slide the pan into the oven and bake for 20 to 25 minutes. Let the muffins cool in the pan on a wire rack for 15 minutes; then remove and serve.

Brownie Bites

SERVES 8 TO 12

Is there anyone who doesn't like brownies? Here's an easy recipe that is sure to hit that chocolate craving.

7 TABLESPOONS BUTTER, PLUS MORE FOR THE PAN
¾ CUP GRANULATED SUGAR
⅓ CUP BROWN SUGAR
½ CUP CHOPPED MILK CHOCOLATE
1 TABLESPOON MAPLE SYRUP
2 EGGS
1 TEASPOON VANILLA EXTRACT
1 CUP ALL-PURPOSE FLOUR
½ TEASPOON BAKING POWDER
2 TABLESPOONS COCOA POWDER

1.   Preheat the oven to 350°F with a rack in the middle position. Butter an 8-inch-square cake pan.

2.   In a saucepan, gently melt the butter, sugar, brown sugar, chocolate, and syrup together over low heat until smooth. Remove the pan from the heat and set aside to cool for 5 to 10 minutes.

3.   Meanwhile, break the eggs into a small bowl and whisk until light and frothy.

4.   Add the beaten eggs, vanilla, flour, baking powder, and cocoa powder to the cooled melted chocolate mixture and mix well. Pour the batter into the prepared pan and bake for 20 to 25 minutes. Remove from the oven and cool in the pan on a wire rack for 20 to 30 minutes before cutting.

Apple Surprise

SERVES 6

Apples for dessert? Sure, why not? A little nutrition in your dessert is allowed.

6 TART APPLES, SUCH AS GRANNY SMITH
¼ CUP RAISINS
¼ CUP COARSELY CHOPPED WALNUTS, PECANS, OR ALMONDS
1 TABLESPOON MAPLE SYRUP
½ TEASPOON GROUND CINNAMON
¼ CUP WATER

1.   Preheat the oven to 375°F.

2.   Cut the top third off of each apple and discard. Carefully remove the core from each apple with a spoon, being sure not to scrape all the way through the center of the apple. Lightly prick the top and sides of the apple with a fork (this prevents the apple's skin from splitting).

3.   In a small bowl, combine the raisins, nuts, syrup, and cinnamon. Divide the mixture evenly among the apples, stuffing it into the holes you made when you removed the cores.

4.   Pour the water into a baking dish and set the apples in the dish, cut-side up. Carefully put the baking dish in the oven and bake until the apples are soft, about 1 hour. Let cool slightly before serving—the apples will be very hot!

Fruity Frozen Yogurt

SERVES 3 TO 4

Perfect for a hot summer day, this treat is quick and easy to make.

2 OVERRIPE BANANAS, PEELED, THINLY SLICED, AND FROZEN
2 CUPS CHOPPED FROZEN PEACHES
½ TEASPOON VANILLA EXTRACT
⅓ CUP PLAIN YOGURT

1. Place the frozen bananas and peaches in an unplugged food processor. Plug in the machine and process the fruit until smooth.

2. Turn off the machine and add the vanilla and yogurt; process again until thoroughly mixed. Unplug the machine and scoop the fruit-yogurt mixture into bowls.

Dessert

Crunchy Crisp

SERVES 8

This is a recipe that goes back for generations! Make it the next time your grandparents come by, and it's sure to earn a few smiles.

5 TO 6 APPLES, CORED AND CHOPPED

2 TABLESPOONS HONEY

1 TABLESPOON PLUS ¾ CUP ALL-PURPOSE FLOUR

½ TEASPOON GROUND CINNAMON

¾ CUP OLD-FASHIONED OATS

5 TABLESPOONS UNSALTED BUTTER, MELTED

3 TABLESPOONS SUGAR

¼ TEASPOON SALT

1. Preheat the oven to 350°F.

2. In a pie plate, combine the apples, honey, 1 tablespoon of the flour, and the cinnamon and stir well.

3. In a large bowl, combine the remaining ¾ cup flour, the oats, melted butter, sugar, and salt, and stir until the mixture looks like small round pebbles. Pour the crumb mixture over the apple mixture and spread it out until the apples are evenly covered. Carefully put the pie plate in the oven, and bake until the topping is lightly browned and the apples are tender, about 1 hour.

Classic Cookies

YIELDS 24 TO 30 COOKIES

Is there a more familiar and comforting treat than chocolate chip cookies? We don't think so!

1 CUP (2 STICKS) UNSALTED BUTTER, AT ROOM TEMPERATURE

½ CUP GRANULATED SUGAR

1 CUP LIGHT BROWN SUGAR

2 EGGS, AT ROOM TEMPERATURE

1 TABLESPOON VANILLA EXTRACT

1 CUP OLD-FASHIONED OATS

1 CUP ALL-PURPOSE FLOUR

1 CUP WHOLE-WHEAT FLOUR

1 TEASPOON BAKING POWDER

1 TEASPOON BAKING SODA

1 TEASPOON SALT

2 CUPS SEMISWEET CHOCOLATE CHIPS

1. Preheat the oven to 325°F.

2. In a large bowl, using a hand mixer, or in the bowl of a stand mixer fitted with the paddle attachment, combine the butter, sugar, and brown sugar, and mix until smooth. Add the eggs and vanilla and mix well. Add the oats, flours, baking powder, baking soda, and salt, and beat until everything is mixed well. Add the chocolate chips and mix again.

3. Roll pieces of dough into heaping teaspoon-size balls and place them 2 inches apart on a baking sheet. Using your palm, gently press each ball down to flatten it slightly. Bake until the cookies begin to brown at the edges, 12 to 15 minutes. Let cool on the baking sheet on a wire rack. Put the cooled cookies on a plate and repeat with remaining dough, using a cool baking sheet for the new batch.

Rockin' Rice Pudding

SERVES 4 TO 6

This recipe makes a very cool dessert, with subtle flavors and a creamy texture.

½ CUP UNCOOKED RICE

5 CUPS WHOLE MILK

1 CUP SUGAR

1 TEASPOON GROUND CARDAMOM

2 TABLESPOONS SHELLED UNSALTED PISTACHIOS

2 TABLESPOONS RAISINS

1.   Place the rice in a medium bowl and add enough cold water to cover. Swirl the rice around to remove the starch. Pour off the water, and repeat 7 or 8 times until the water is clear when you pour it off.

2.   Next, fill the bowl with enough cold water to cover the rice by 2 inches. Let it soak for 30 minutes. Drain the rice and set aside.

3.   In a saucepan, bring the milk to a boil over medium heat, stirring frequently, 10 to 12 minutes. Add the drained rice and return the mixture to a boil, 1 to 2 minutes. Reduce the heat to maintain a simmer and cook, uncovered, for 30 to 35 minutes. Stir frequently, occasionally mashing the rice with a whisk. The rice will absorb the milk as it cooks and thickens.

4.   After almost all the milk has been absorbed and the rice is tender, add the sugar and ground cardamom. Stir well to combine the ingredients. Pour the rice pudding into a bowl, cover, and chill for 1 hour. Divide the rice pudding among individual serving bowls, sprinkle each bowl with pistachios and raisins, and serve.

Caramel Pecan Pie

SERVES 8

Pecans and caramel are a wonderful mix, so put them together in this yummy pie.

36 INDIVIDUALLY WRAPPED CARAMELS, UNWRAPPED

¼ CUP (½ STICK) BUTTER

¼ CUP MILK

¾ CUP SUGAR

3 EGGS

½ TEASPOON VANILLA EXTRACT

¼ TEASPOON SALT

½ CUP CHOPPED PECANS

ONE 9-INCH UNBAKED PREPARED PIE CRUST

1.   Preheat the oven to 350°F.

2.   In a medium saucepan, combine the caramels, butter, and milk. Cook over low heat, stirring frequently, until smooth. Remove from the heat and set aside.

3.   In a large bowl, combine the sugar, eggs, vanilla, and salt. Gradually stir in the melted caramel mixture. Stir in the pecans. Pour the filling into the unbaked pie crust. Bake for 45 to 50 minutes, or until the crust is golden brown. Let cool on a wire rack, until the filling is firm, before cutting into wedges and serving.

Bread-in-a-Bowl Pudding

SERVES 6

Bread pudding is one of the most popular desserts in restaurants around the world. Make this recipe and find out why.

6 SLICES DAY-OLD BREAD

2 TABLESPOONS BUTTER, MELTED

½ CUP RAISINS

4 EGGS, BEATEN

2 CUPS MILK

¾ CUP SUGAR

1 TEASPOON GROUND CINNAMON

1 TEASPOON VANILLA EXTRACT

1. Preheat the oven to 350°F.

2. Break the bread into small pieces and place them in an 8-inch-square baking pan. Drizzle the melted butter over the bread and sprinkle in the raisins.

3. In a medium bowl, combine the eggs, milk, sugar, cinnamon, and vanilla. Beat until well combined. Pour the egg mixture over the bread, and lightly push down with a fork until the bread is covered and soaking up the egg mixture. Bake for 45 minutes, or until the top springs back when lightly tapped.

Going Bananas

MAKES 1 LOAF

This banana bread can be a great snack or just the perfect finish to a meal. It's even good for you!

OIL, FOR THE PAN

1 CUP ALL-PURPOSE FLOUR

½ CUP WHOLE-WHEAT FLOUR

1½ TEASPOONS BAKING SODA

½ TEASPOON SALT

4 OVERRIPE BANANAS, PEELED

1 CUP SUGAR

½ CUP (1 STICK) UNSALTED BUTTER, MELTED AND COOLED

2 EGGS, AT ROOM TEMPERATURE

2 TEASPOONS VANILLA EXTRACT

½ CUP CHOPPED PECANS

1.   Preheat the oven to 350°F. Using a paper towel and a little oil, lightly grease a 9-by-5-inch loaf pan.

2.   In a medium bowl, combine the flours, baking soda, and salt and mix well. Set aside.

3.   In a large bowl, combine the bananas and sugar, and mash together with a fork or whisk until the mixture is completely smooth. Add the butter, eggs, and vanilla and mix well. Add the flour mixture, a little at a time, and mix well. Add the pecans and mix again.

4.   Pour the mixture into the prepared loaf pan and carefully put it in the oven. Bake until firm in the center, about 1 hour. Set aside to cool before slicing and serving.

Berries and Cream

MAKES 1 QUART

You can make this dessert any time of the year—but during the summer, when strawberries are at their peak, is the best! You'll need an ice-cream maker for this one.

ONE 14-OUNCE CAN SWEETENED CONDENSED MILK

ONE 5-OUNCE CAN EVAPORATED MILK

2 TABLESPOONS SUGAR

½ CUP WHOLE MILK

1 POUND FRESH STRAWBERRIES, HULLED, OR ONE 16-OUNCE PACKAGE
    FROZEN STRAWBERRIES, THAWED

2 TABLESPOONS LEMON JUICE

¼ TEASPOON SALT

1.   In a large bowl, whisk together the condensed milk, evaporated milk, sugar, and whole milk until blended. Cover and chill for 30 minutes.

2.   In an unplugged blender, combine the strawberries, lemon juice, and salt. Plug in the machine and blend until smooth. Turn off and unplug the blender, and carefully spoon the strawberry mixture into the chilled milk mixture. Stir well to combine.

3.   Pour the ice cream base into the freezer container of a 1-quart electric ice-cream maker, and freeze according to the manufacturer's instructions. (Instructions and freezing times will vary.) Remove the container with the ice cream from the ice-cream maker, and place it in the freezer for 15 minutes. Transfer the ice cream to a storage container and freeze until firm, 1 to 1½ hours, depending on how firm you like your ice cream!

Luscious Lemon Bars

MAKES ABOUT 20 BARS

This recipe blends sweet and tart into perfect lemony bars of goodness.

BUTTER, FOR THE PAN
2¼ CUPS ALL-PURPOSE FLOUR
½ CUP CONFECTIONERS' SUGAR, PLUS MORE FOR DUSTING
1 CUP (2 STICKS) BUTTER, CUT INTO PIECES
4 LARGE EGGS
2 CUPS GRANULATED SUGAR
1 TEASPOON GRATED LEMON ZEST
⅓ CUP FRESH LEMON JUICE
½ TEASPOON BAKING POWDER

1. Preheat the oven to 350°F. Line the bottom and sides of a 13-by-9-inch baking pan with heavy-duty aluminum foil, leaving about 3 inches of foil overhanging the edges of the pan, and lightly butter the foil.

2. In a large bowl, stir together 2 cups of the flour and the confectioners' sugar. Mix in the butter using a fork until crumbly. Press the mixture into an even layer over the bottom of the prepared pan. Bake for 20 to 25 minutes, or until lightly browned. Remove from the oven but leave the oven on.

3. In a large bowl, whisk the eggs until smooth; then whisk in the granulated sugar, lemon zest, and lemon juice.

4. In a separate bowl, stir together the baking powder and remaining ¼ cup flour; then whisk it into the egg mixture. Pour the mixture over the hot baked crust. Bake for 25 minutes or until the filling is set. Let cool for 30 minutes in the pan; then lift from the pan, using the foil sides as handles. Set on a wire rack and let cool completely, about 30 minutes.

5. Remove the foil, dust with confectioners' sugar, and cut into bars.

Measurements

Cooking Measurements

1 tablespoon (tbsp)	=	3 teaspoons (tsp)
$\frac{1}{16}$ cup	=	1 tablespoon
$\frac{1}{8}$ cup	=	2 tablespoons
$\frac{1}{6}$ cup	=	2 tablespoons + 2 teaspoons
$\frac{1}{4}$ cup	=	4 tablespoons
$\frac{1}{3}$ cup	=	5 tablespoons + 1 teaspoon
$\frac{3}{8}$ cup	=	6 tablespoons
$\frac{1}{2}$ cup	=	8 tablespoons
$\frac{2}{3}$ cup	=	10 tablespoons + 2 teaspoons
$\frac{3}{4}$ cup	=	12 tablespoons
1 cup	=	48 teaspoons
1 cup	=	16 tablespoons
8 fluid ounces (fl oz)	=	1 cup
1 pint (pt)	=	2 cups
1 quart (qt)	=	2 pints
4 cups	=	1 quart
1 gallon (gal)	=	4 quarts
16 ounces (oz)	=	1 pound (lb)
1 milliliter (mL)	=	1 cubic centimeter (cc)
1 inch (in)	=	2.54 centimeters (cm)

Source: U.S. Department of Agriculture (USDA)

U.S.–Metric Cooking Conversions

U.S. TO METRIC

Capacity

⅕ teaspoon (tsp)	=	1 milliliter (mL)
1 teaspoon	=	5 milliliters
1 tablespoon (tbsp)	=	15 milliliters
1 fluid oz	=	30 milliliters
⅕ cup	=	47 milliliters
1 cup	=	237 milliliters
2 cups (1 pt)	=	473 milliliters
4 cups (1 qt)	=	0.95 liter
4 quarts (1 gal)	=	3.8 liters

Weight

1 oz	=	28 grams
1 pound	=	454 grams

METRIC TO U.S.

Capacity

1 milliliter	=	⅕ teaspoon
5 milliliters	=	1 teaspoon
15 milliliters	=	1 tablespoon
100 milliliters	=	3.4 fluid ounces
240 milliliters	=	1 cup
1 liter	=	34 fluid ounces
1 liter	=	4.2 cups
1 liter	=	2.1 pints
1 liter	=	1.06 quarts
1 liter	=	0.26 gallon

Weight

1 gram	=	0.035 ounce
100 grams	=	3.5 ounces
500 grams	=	1.10 pounds
1 kilogram	=	2.205 pounds
1 kilogram	=	35 ounces

Recipe Index

Index

CPSIA information can be obtained
at www.ICGtesting.com
Printed in the USA
LVHW01s1429180918
590303LV00002B/2/P